Interferei
on the
Airwaves

Ireland, the Media, and the Broadcasting Ban

Part 1
A Shameful Anniversary
by Mike Jempson

Part 2.
A Catalogue of Censorship, 1959-1993
by Liz Curtis

Published by the

with the co-sponsorship of

Interference on the Airwaves
Ireland, the Media and the Broadcasting Ban

A Shameful Anniversary © Mike Jempson, 1993

A Catalogue of Censorship, 1959-1993 © Liz Curtis, 1993

ISBN 1 898240 01 9

Liz Curtis is a freelance journalist and researcher. She is the author of *Ireland: The Propaganda War* (Pluto 1984) and *Nothing But the Same Old Story: The Roots of Anti-Irish Racism* (Information on Ireland 1984). Her latest publication is *Making Advances: What to do about Sexual Harassment at Work* (BBC Books 1993).

Mike Jempson is a freelance journalist of Irish descent, and a member of the CPBF National Council. He writes and lectures on media policy issues. His publications this year include *Freedom & Responsibility of the Press*; *Human Rights and the UK: The Challenge to Government*; and *The Centenary History of the Musicians' Union*.

The NUJ is co-sponsoring publication of this booklet because we believe that it is a useful contribution to the debate about censorship and the future of Ireland.

INTERFERENCE WITH THE AIRWAVES
Ireland, the Media, and the Broadcasting Ban

Introduction

Censorship is an abuse of power, invariably used to cover up that which the powerful find distressing or threatening.

In a democracy it is a function of the media to expose wrong-doing and call the powerful to account. That function cannot be fulfilled when the media succumb to censorship.

It is a function of trades unions to defend the rights of workers against the abuse of power by their employers. That function is also undermined when the law is used to hobble unions and prevent collective action.

In Britain today we suffer both from censorship and repressive anti-union legislation. Yet despite the hurdles place in their way, the media unions have taken the firmest stand against censorship and in favour of the journalist's right to report and the public's right to know.

That is why the National Union of Journalists, backed by the broad-casting technicians' union BECTU, is pursuing the British Government to the European Court over the infamous Broadcasting Ban imposed in 1988, and why they and many other unions have given support over the years to the work of the Campaign for Press & Broadcasting Freedom.

The CPBF has regularly challenged censorship by publishing banned material. It has been in the forefront of efforts to alert the public to the distortion and censorship which is routinely applied by the British media to coverage of 'The Troubles' in Northern Ireland.

The Broadcasting Ban further restricts the ability of broadcasters to supply accurate and comprehensive coverage about a conflict that has cost over 3,000 lives in the last 24 years.

The CPBF and the NUJ are marking the fifth anniversary with this review of British television coverage of Ireland. Part 1 examines the circumstances surrounding the Broadcasting Ban; Part 2 catalogues the programmes that have been banned, censored or delayed since 1959.

Neither the CPBF nor the NUJ takes sides in the conflict itself. We reaffirm our opposition to political censorship and the Broadcasting Ban, and defend the right of all citizens to be fully informed about what is being done in their name.

Tony Lennon
Chair, CPBF National Council
President, BECTU

Jacob Ecclestone
Deputy General Secretary
National Union of Journalists

A SHAMEFUL ANNIVERSARY

by Mike Jempson

1. Britain in the dock

Britain has the worst record of any European country for breaches of the European Convention on Human Rights. Many of these findings by the European Court relate to the British Government's handling of the political problems in the North of Ireland.

As the media contemplate the fifth anniversary of the October 1988 'Broadcasting Ban' which imposed unprecedented restrictions on the public's right to know about what is happening there, the British Government faces several new charges in Europe.

In three separate actions, six members of the National Union of Journalists, Sinn Fein Councillor Mitchell McLaughlin and former MP Bernadette McAliskey, are challenging the legitimacy of the ban.

And in the summer of 1993, the European Commission on Human Rights acknowledged that Britain had a case to answer in an action brought by relatives of three Irish Republican Army (IRA) volunteers shot dead by the Special Air Service (SAS) in Gibraltar in March 1988.

Media management

In January 1988, two months before the killings, the Foreign and Commonwealth Office issued a lengthy intelligence briefing to the European (but not the British) media entitled 'The Provisional IRA : International Contacts outside the United States'.

It explained how the IRA drew support and comfort from "conservative Irish expatriate(s)" and "political extremists" including Communists, Trotskyists, anti-Western groups, anarchists and radical feminists throughout Eastern and Western Europe, the Middle East, Latin America and, of course, Libya.

By naming names (some of which it would later have to apologise for and remove), dates and places, the Government implied the existence of an organised international network of IRA sympathisers.

Although marked "not to be construed or quoted as an expression of Government policy", the document was a classic example of media

5

management. Marketing this conspiracy theory at that time had two functions: to assist in gaining the co-operation of French and Spanish security services in the secret military operation against an IRA active service unit that was already under way; and to 'soften-up' Britain's neighbours for its spectacular consequences.

In the aftermath of the Gibraltar killings much effort was made by the Government, and its sympathisers in the media - notably the *Sunday Times* and the *Sun* - to rubbish the Thames TV programme *'Death on the Rock'* which offered a rather different version of what happened to that given by the authorities.

In an extraordinary move Lord Windlesham, a Tory former Northern Ireland Minister, was appointed by Thames TV to investigate the making of the programme. He himself then became the subject of vilification when his report exonerated the programme-makers.

A similar fate had befallen others who attempted to blow the whistle on the clandestine activities of the police and security forces in the North of Ireland. Carefully placed 'leaks' encouraged the media to label them 'mad, bad or dangerous to know'.

Police chief John Stalker found himself suspended and under criminal investigation in 1986, at the height of his own official investigation into the fatal shootings of six unarmed Catholics by members of the Royal Ulster Constabulary (RUC). Stalker was never charged and resigned in disgust.

Former Army Press Officer Colin Wallace maintains that the secret service 'framed' him for manslaughter after he was unfairly dismissed from his post in the North of Ireland, ostensibly for leaking information to a journalist in 1975. His military intelligence function included supplying the press with, often false, stories. His real 'crime' had been to object to a security service cover-up of sexual abuse at the Kincora Boys Home in Belfast, and to Operation Clockwork Orange - a secret plot to destabilise the then Labour Government.
Wallace's claim of unfair dismissal was eventually upheld 16 years later, but only after he had spent six years in gaol and the Government had spent millions trying to suppress 'Spycatcher' by Peter Wright, another intelligence officer's version of the Clockwork Orange Plot.

Captain Fred Holroyd, a former military intelligence officer, has been dogged by allegations of mental instability since he tried to go public about his covert role in the North of Ireland. To silence him the authorities forced Holroyd into a psychiatric unit before 'letting him go', and have used that incarceration to discredit his testimony.

6

Secret history

For generations British Governments have jealously guarded media access to information about the situation.

Restrictions on the release of 'public records' about Britain's management of the North of Ireland and its relationship with the rest of Ireland far exceed the 30-year embargo placed on most official documents.

It will be another 40 years before the public can begin to read about 'RUC and Military Activities in Northern Ireland, 1937-1959', or official reports about the IRA's 1958-59 campaign and Sinn Fein's position during the 1959 General Election. Information about Stormont Castle Accommodation (1922-41) and the report of the Belfast Union (Workhouse) 1934 remain under a 100-year embargo.

Public records have revealed that the Northern Ireland Cabinet met twice at Stormont in 1959 to discuss the first of Alan Whicker's 10-minute tele-portraits about life in the Six Counties for the BBC's *Tonight* programme.

Following protests by the then Minister of Finance, Captain Terence O'Neill, the BBC agreed to allow its National Governor for Northern Ireland, Ritchie McKee, to preview the remaining reports in the series. They were never broadcast.

It was a sinister concession which set a pattern from which broadcasters have yet to escape, as Liz Curtis's list of banned and censored programmes illustrates.

2. Before the ban

Silence about embarrassing issues is a great comfort to politicians. Apart from a brief flurry of outrage at the IRA's 'border campaign' in the late 1950s, the media obliged for many years, especially when it came to the border issue which is at the centre of the conflict in the North of Ireland.

Since 1921 six of Ireland's 32 counties have been governed as part of the United Kingdom. (There were nine counties in the ancient Irish province of Ulster, three of which remain part of the Republic of Ireland.) With a built-in Protestant majority, the Unionists who had brought about this partition governed a sectarian society.
They held sway even in the media, making it fairly easy to keep the lid on any attempt to expose the inequalities faced by Catholics to the glare of external public attention.
In the late Sixties, inspired by those struggling for Black emancipation in the United States, a Northern Ireland civil rights movement emerged seeking publicity for their demands by organising peaceful protest marches.
At the time few people in Britain knew that some of their so-called fellow citizens did not even have the vote and were routinely discriminated against in the housing and jobs market solely on the basis of their (Catholic) religion. In 1969, 21-year-old People's Democracy candidate Bernadette Devlin (now McAliskey) was elected to Parliament and came to Westminster to speak for the dispossessed minority.

It was the shocking TV images of police attacking unarmed, peaceful civil rights marchers that sent the first tremors of anxiety through the establishment. In America the horrors of the Vietnam war had been brought home through TV, turning public opinion against the war, boosting the peace-movement, and eventually forcing the US to abandon its adventure in Indo-China.

Since control of most images was then in the hands of what has been described as a 'Unionist media mafia' in Belfast, it was possible to put a gloss, or a damper, on interpretations of what happened after British troops

8

arrived to protect the Catholic, nationalist minority from a Protestant, unionist backlash.

The RUC and their auxiliaries, the B-Specials, had joined forces with the mob in attacks on Catholic ghettos where people looked to the IRA to protect them.

By 1971 it was clear that the emergent 'Provisional' IRA, formed after a split with the Official IRA a year earlier, was determined to meet force with force and the nationalist community was not prepared to allow a return to the corrupt *status quo*.

Internment was introduced to lock up the paramilitaries. But when the cameras captured British troops opening fire on a civil rights march in Derry killing 14 unarmed people on 'Bloody Sunday' (10 January 1972), the time had come for more sophisticated media management techniques if the 'Vietnam-syndrome' were to be avoided.

Reference upwards

Both the BBC and the commercial broadcasters enforced a system of 'reference upwards', requiring reporters and editors to seek permission and advice from their superiors before embarking on stories connected with the North of Ireland.

The upper limit of the system extended beyond the media institutions, and incorporated 'guidance' from the political and military authorities. At the time appointments to the BBC staff were subject to external security vetting - something we are now assured no longer happens.

Meanwhile the politicians sanctioned the 'psy-ops' (psychological operations) programme which encouraged military intelligence officers like Colin Wallace to manipulate the media by feeding their journalist contacts with misinformation.

By the late Seventies British broadcasters were becoming more and more circumspect about what programmes could or should be made.

In September 1979, soon after the election of Margaret Thatcher's Tory Government, the BBC's Panorama team got the go-ahead for a study of the Provisional IRA. Tipped off to visit Carrickmore, a village just a few miles from major security forces emplacements, they filmed a roadblock set up by hooded IRA members.

When news of the incident reached Mrs Thatcher the matter was raised in Cabinet and British politicians and the Press went on the warpath against Panorama. Following a Commons debate on 8 November, the Director of Public Prosecutions ordered a police investigation, and the BBC began its own inquiry. The police demanded and were given access to untransmitted footage of the incident.

On 16 November Panorama Editor Roger Bolton was sacked. NUJ members immediately acted in his defence, and within a week he was reinstated with a reprimand.
Bolton later left the BBC and joined Thames TV, where he would feel the wrath of the Prime Minister again for making 'Death on the Rock'. His Panorama film on the Provisionals was never finished.
The incident was a watershed in the fraught relationhsip between Government and the media over Ireland.

During the Thatcher years the Cabinet became increasingly paranoid about the broadcast media, and took to more direct intervention, not least because of growing support for the Provisionals within an ever more alienated nationalist community.

Political action

In 1981 prisoners from several republican groups went on hunger strike demanding recognition of their political status as prisoners of war.

The withdrawal of 'special category' status had already led to three years of prison protests and Thatcher remained intransigent, challenging Provisional Sinn Fein, a political party, to test its strength at the polls.

Hunger striker Bobby Sands was elected to the Westminster Parliament before he became the first to die. But what really appalled the Government was Sinn Fein's ability to sustain electoral support beyond the immediate aftermath of ten prisoners starving themselves to death.

At the 1983 General Election Sinn Fein polled 13.4% of all votes cast in the North of Ireland. In the 1985 local elections Sinn Fein had the support of almost 12% of the electorate (43% of the nationalist vote) and 59 Sinn Fein councillors were elected. Sinn Fein took the chair of Omagh District Council, where it was the largest party, and was joint largest party in Fermanagh and Magherafelt. At the 1987 General Election Sinn Fein took 13.5% of the votes in the constituencies it contested.

The Government's response to this upsurge in successful political engagement was the Elected Authorities (NI) Act of 1988, which banned anyone convicted of a criminal offence from holding elected office.

Since many leading Sinn Fein political activists had served prison sentences, it was clear at whom the measure was aimed.

Those expressing support for terrorism or for a proscribed organisation were disqualified from holding office for five years, and to take their seats successful candidates now had to publicly declare their rejection of political violence.

Sections of the republican community welcomed the opportunity to build a public, political base. But the measure undermined the credibility of all those within the nationalist community who argued for sustained political activity as a prerequisite for eventual suspension of the guerrilla tactics of the Provisional IRA.

Young people who might otherwise have considered volunteering for the IRA had been encouraged to engage in constructive community politics instead. It was difficult to sustain enthusiasm for the political option when it seemed to be frustrated at every turn.

The Thatcher administration had been warned by its Standing Advisory Commission on Human Rights that devising "artificial means to exclude councillors from local politics" was "fundamentally wrong" and "cannot hope to succeed in the long-term".

A significant section of the nationalist community was now being told that its particular brand of local politics was not acceptable to Westminster.

Then in October 1988 the Government introduced the Broadcasting Ban to remind everyone else that no credibility should be given to ideas and opinions which did not meet with the Cabinet's approval.

As if to underline this contempt for public debate, the Home Secretary used powers conferred by existing broadcasting legislation to issue an edict. When the Commons did debate the Ban (2 November 1988) the Government relied on its massive majority to claim Parliamentary approval (by 243 votes to 179) for perhaps the most insidious act of political censorship in peacetime.

BEFORE YOU TELL US ABOUT YOUR LOST BUDGIE, MRS O'FLANEL, I MUST JUST ASK IF YOU'RE A SUPPORTER OF SINN FEIN.....?

3. The 'Ban'

When Douglas Hurd, then Home Secretary in the Thatcher Cabinet, announced the ban on 19 October 1988 he invoked executive powers to determine what may be broadcast contained in the Broadcasting Act 1981 and Clause 13(4) of the BBC's Licence and Agreement.

His formal notice to the Independent Broadcasting Authority (IBA) read :

'1. In pursuance of section 29(3) of the Broadcasting Act 1981, I hereby require the Independent Broadcasting Authority to refrain from broadcasting any matter which consists of or includes -

any words spoken, whether in the course of an interview or discussion or otherwise, by a person who appears or is heard on the programme in which the matter is broadcast where

a) the person speaking the words represents or purports to represent an organisation specified in paragraph 2 below, or b) the worlds support or solicit or invite support for such an organisation, other than any matter specified in paragraph 3 below.

2. The organisations referred to in paragraph 1 above are -

a) any organisation which is for the time being a proscribed organisation for the purposes of the Prevention of Terrorism (Temporary Provisions) Act 1984 or the Northern Ireland (Emergency Provisions) Act 1978; and

b) Sinn Fein, Republican Sinn Fein and the Ulster Defence Association.

3. The matter excluded from paragraph 1 above is any words spoken -

a) in the course of proceedings in parliament, or

b) by or in support of a candidate at a parliamentary, European Parliamentary or local election pending that election.'

Legislation referred to in para. 1 lists the following organisations:

The Irish Republican Army

Cumann na mBan *(the republican women's section)*

Fianna na hEireann *(the republican youth section)*

The Red Hand Commando *(unionist paramilitaries)*

Saor Eire *(Free Ireland - a defunct republican group)*
The Ulster Freedom Fighters *(unionist paramilitaries)*
The Ulster Volunteer Force *(unionist paramilitaries)*
The Irish National Liberation Army *(a republican splinter group)*

Since the Ban was imposed the Ulster Defence Association has been proscribed by the British Government. The UDA now is barred from direct access to the airwaves under the provisions of para. 2(a) rather than 2(b).

The same empowering clause used to impose the ban on commercial broadcasters now appears in the Broadcasting Act 1990 Sec.10(3), under which the restrictions still apply.

This power had been used only five times previously.

When it was granted a Royal Charter in 1927 the BBC was directed not to broadcast its own opinion on current affairs or matters of public policy. This 'objectivity' condition also now applies to commercial broadcasters.

At the same time the BBC was ordered not to broadcast matters of political, industrial or religious controversy - a ludicrous condition withdrawn the following year.

In 1955 all broadcasters were directed to abstain from comment on matters scheduled to be discussed in Parliament during the 14 days prior to the debate. The restriction was subsequently withdrawn.

In the same year the Churchill administration also instructed the BBC not to transmit party political broadcasts other than those approved by the main political parties. (Commercial companies were only allowed to transmit those broadcast by the BBC.) This restriction remained in force for ten years.

In 1964 all broadcasters were instructed by the Labour Government not to make use of subliminal techniques.

4. The Reader's Digest approach to politics

Even today, the Department of National Heritage (DNH), which has since taken over responsibility for broadcasting from the Home Office, insists that the reason for the Ban was Cabinet anger at broadcasts involving proponents of political violence.

"The Government believes that organisations and individuals who support the use of violence for political ends in Britain do not share the same rights of access to the airwaves as anyone else," says a DNH spokesperson. "It is unacceptable for relatives of victims to have to endure seeing people justifying terrorism. The Government believed that the time had come to put a stop to it."

Strangely the DNH now insists that the measure was designed to put broadcasters on the same 'level playing field' as print journalists (who are not affected by the ban), and was aimed at clarifying the position of broadcasters *vis a vis* those who condone or commit acts of political violence in Britain.

Challenged by the NUJ in the High Court in 1989, the Government had defended its action by explaining that the appearance of 'terrorists and their apologists' on TV:

'afforded (them) undeserved publicity, which was contrary to the public interest...;

'tended to increase (their) standing and create the false impression that support for terrorism is itself a legitimate political opinion'; and

'were intended to have, and in some cases did have, the effect of intimidating some of those at whom they were directed'.

The only evidence cited in justification for this last rationale was a broadcast statement by Sinn Fein MP Gerry Adams after the bombing of the home of Sir Kenneth Bloomfield, head of the Northern Ireland Civil Service earlier in 1988.

The Government had to acknowledge in court that the particular broadcast featured Adams commenting on a statement issued by the

14

Provisional IRA warning that other civil servants might become targets, and as such would not have been covered by the Ban had it been in operation at the time.

'Head we win, tails they lose'

At the time of its imposition Douglas Hurd's justification for the ban rested in part on the results of a MORI poll conducted for the *Reader's Digest* earlier in 1988 which suggested that 69% of those interviewed disapproved of terrorist organisations being allowed to express their views on TV. Yet neither the PLO nor the ANC, which were regularly described as terrorist organisations at the time, were covered by the ban.

In his statement to the Commons Hurd claimed that "the occasional appearance of representatives of paramilitary organisations and their political wings" had "caused widespread offence to viewers and listeners".

In the same breath Hurd also asserted that "terrorists themselves draw support and sustenance from access to radio and television".

This 'heads-we-win, tails-they-lose' logic was supposed to reassure those who saw the measure as an act of political censorship. Indeed the government was at pains to stress that it was not 'banning' anything, merely restricting access to the airwaves.

"This step is no criticism of (broadcasters)." Hurd told MPs. "What concerns us is the use made of broadcasting facilities by supporters of terrorism. This is not a restriction on reporting. It is a restriction on direct appearances by those who use or support violence."

> *Contrary to the impression given by the Home Secretary, the only time a self-declared IRA member had been interviewed on screen by British broadcasters was after the Birmingham bombings of 1974.*
> *In 1979 a hooded, unidentified member of the Irish National Liberation Army (INLA) was interviewed on British TV after the assassination of Airey Neave MP in an explosion at the House of Commons car park.*

Commentators close to government circles claimed at the time of the ban that Mrs Thatcher had wanted to introduce even more draconian measures ever since the INLA murder of Airey Neave, her friend and confidant.

Wiser counsels had prevailed, but after the IRA ambushed 40 British soldiers at Ballygawley on 20 August 1988, killing eight of them, Mrs Thatcher had cut short a holiday to demand 'options' in reprisal. A Security Review Conference on 24 August considered the re-introduction of internment and proscription of Sinn Fein, but plumped instead for the Ban coupled with new secret intelligence and military operations.

Thatcher would later acknowledge both that the British Government

15

was engaged in a war (an admission rarely made in all the rhetoric about 'The Troubles'), and that civil liberties were indeed at stake (a concession most often denied by the Government when the measure is criticised on such grounds).

"To beat off your enemy in a war," she said. "You have to suspend your civil liberties for a time." *(Times 26.10.88)*

Media Union Leaders march against the Broadcasting Ban on the second anniversary, on the 19th October 1989.
(Left to right: Harry Conton, NUJ;
            Doug Hearn BETA
            and Alan Sapper ACTT)

5. First reactions

Acres of coverage were devoted the Ban in the national press on October 20, and leader columns signalled each paper's attitude.

Predictably the *Daily Express* and the *Daily Telegraph* welcomed the Ban the next day, both wishing the Government had gone further. The *Telegraph* leader presciently warned that its effectiveness should be 'gauged against its impact abroad, where it will be seen as another example of Britain's heavy hand in Ulster'.

The *Daily Mail* also favoured the Ban, but allowed space to dissenting comment. Two days later its sister paper, the *Mail on Sunday* published an extraordinary broadside against the Ban headlined

'A SORRY DAY FOR BRITISH LIBERTY
Bulldog spirit is more than enough to crush IRA
TV owes people of Ulster a fair deal

There was cautious support for the Ban from *The Times*, but its News International stable-mate *Today* was opposed, and there was a curious silence from the down-market *Sun*, though it has seldom flinched from making clear its position on Ireland. A year later it would declare:

'We've said it before and we'll say it again: Buying Irish produce is tantamount to financing the IRA to murder Britons.'
(*Sun* Editorial, 22 Nov 1989)

The tabloid *Daily Star* and the Labour-supporting *Daily Mirror* also had no immediate editorial comment but the *Daily Mirror*, which at the time favoured the withdrawal of British troops later came out against the ban.

That was the line taken on 20 October 1988 by the *Financial Times* - which found the Government's position 'implausible'; and the two 'liberal' broadsheets - *The Guardian*, which saw the ban as the 'thin end of a wedge'; and *The Independent,* which demanded that a democratic Government should trust the public's 'right to judge for themselves'.

The Communist daily *Morning Star* also raised objections to the Ban.

In a highly critical Editorial the following Sunday, *The Observer* made the connection between the Ban, the ending of a suspect's right to silence and the outlawing of trades unions at GCHQ.

The People linked it to the tactics employed by the Eastern Bloc and South Africa, and to the *Spycatcher* debacle, declaring the Government 'WRONG, WRONG, WRONG'.

The *Sunday Times* contained three pieces opposing the Ban but made no editorial comment, while the *Sunday Telegraph* carried a signed editorial by Peregrine Worsthorne welcoming the measure and attacking those who opposed it.

In America the *Wall Street Journal* ('one of the stupidest moves the Tory Government has ever made'), the *New York Times* ('Britain's good name... tarnished by a Conservative government') and the *Washington Post* ('the restrictions are wrong and... counter-productive') were at one with the Cuban government press agency *Prensa Latina* in condemning the Ban.

And in South Africa the Johannesburg *Citizen* warned that Britain would now find it hard to condemn South Africa's censorship laws. The *apartheid* regime had been one of the first foreign governments to applaud the British administration for its action.

However, despite statements of protest from all the main broadcasting authorities, it was immediately clear that the government had won the battle without a fight. Although they all maintain their 'principled opposition' to this day, there was not the slightest indication from broadcasting executives of united action to defeat the Ban.

6. Accommodating the Ban

If the Government still seems confused about precisely what its original intentions were, there was certainly confusion among broadcasters in the days following the Hurd edict. Interpretation of the Home Secretary's intentions was left to the broadcasters. Their legal advisors erred, as always, on the side of caution.

On 24 October 1988 Don Christopher from C4's legal services department issued an advice note to producers:

'It does not matter whether or not the word spoken concern the aims of the organisation in question, or indeed anything to do with the politics of Northern Ireland. The ban would also cover anyone who 'purports' to represent one of the organisations even if he does so without justification or authority.

'The ban is not limited to material produced or recorded after 19th October. It would cover any material recorded at any time in the past - for example, newsreel footage shot before the creation of the Republic of Ireland.

"This part of the ban would also seem to prevent either the use of mute footage of the representative, together with either a verbatim or paraphrased voice-over describing what he is saying or what he has said.

'The second part of the ban has an even wider effect. This prevents **any** programme item which consists of, or **includes**, any words, spoken by **anyone** who is seen or heard in the item, if those words 'support or solicit or invite support' for one of the listed organisations. This would appear to be so even if the offending words are accompanied by opposing statements from the same or another speaker or source...'

It went on to say :

'As this part of the ban concerns the inclusion of offending words, spoken by 'a person', it would appear also to apply to equally to works of fiction, whatever their provenance or theme.'

And ended :

'By a curious omission, there would appear to be no exemption for fair and accurate reports of proceedings in open court, a hitherto unchallenged requisite for the principle of open justice.'

The next day, after consultation with the Home Office, both the BBC and ITN issued new guidelines which announced that "genuine" (ITN's gloss) works of fiction were exempt from the Ban.

'Actors playing characters are speaking someone else's words, not their own,' explained the BBC document.

However, actuality from all parliaments throughout the world, except Westminster, would be covered by the Ban, as would actuality from any court in the world (except Britain where such coverage is forbidden by law).

Rewriting history

One of the most sinister notes in these fresh interpretation indicated that history would indeed have to be rewritten:

'Library material is covered. Comments which offend the order do not have to have been recently made." (BBC)

'There is no exemption from the terms of the Notice for historical documentaries, or for recordings of persons who are now dead.' (ITN)

Even Conor Cruise O'Brien, architect of similar censorship legislation in the Irish Republic, has condemned as 'ridiculous' the possibility that such world figures as Ireland's former President Eamonn de Valera and Nobel Peace Prize-winner Sean MacBride, both deceased, might be barred from speaking their own words in archive footage.

The slant placed on Anglo-Irish history in schools has rarely acknowledged an Irish perspective. Under this interpretation broadcasters might now feel obliged to ensure that their British audiences were not upset or contaminated by hearing those who fought for and won independence for Ireland over seventy years ago. Such restrictions apply to no other former colony or corner of the defunct British Empire.

In his three page advice note faxed to all BBC editors, John Wilson, Controller Editorial Policy, drew attention to the way the Ban would affect programmes "especially in Northern Ireland".

'To take an example : the Chairman of Strabane Council, who is Sinn Fein, can appear in programmes **to represent the Council**.*(his emphasis)* He can speak about Council business, decisions made, problems faced, so long as he does not proclaim Sinn Fein. It is accepted that such people are not always representing their organisation even when speaking about their public duties. They cannot be held to represent their organisation in all their daily activities. Some will be regarded as private. There will be difficult borderline cases to be decided case by case depending on the context and the words spoken. Don't hesitate to consult.'

In other words legally-elected councillors might be allowed to talk about their own homes and the Council's housing policy, but not their party's housing policy.

The BBC advice note explained that reported speech 'is not now restricted' (an indication that the Corporation had been over-zealous in its initial interpretation of the ban).

Editors were reminded that 'pictures showing someone speaking but with the words given in voice-over are permitted' (a former BBC Vice-Chair Mark Bonham Carter would later comment that "deaf people who can lip read are exempt from the ban"), and that while political commentators may not 'speak words of support of their own, they can quote any of the organisations or any other sources for purposes of explanation or argument.'

*Two years later, in November 1990, TV reporter Peter Taylor would expose the ludicrous nature of this ruling in his remarkable film about the Maze prison. In the programme a convicted IRA member was able to speak his own words to explain his **personal** involvement with the paramilitaries straight to camera, but had to rely upon sub-titles when he was filmed **representing** IRA prisoners in a discussion with prison staff about the size of sausage rolls.*

Under the ban, opportunities for members of the public to air their views free from editorial control are fraught with problems, as Wilson's advice note explained:

'Phone-ins and other live programmes should continue to be live. At the same time (editors/presenters) must be ready to stop anyone who starts to speak in support of any of the (banned) organisations. If necessary, warnings can be given on the programme and any transgressor cut off quickly. If a programme has reason to be concerned about a prospective or likely participant such a person should not be taken live, which may well mean not at all.'

How were producers and presenters to tell ? If ever there were a recipe for self-censorship this was it. A local radio station in Birmingham, BRMB, immediately cancelled a planned phone-in with former-MP Bernadette McAliskey, who does not support the IRA.

Four years later McAliskey would be 'voiced-over' on a BBC-commissioned independently-produced TV panel discussion, Nation. During that broadcast two unidentified members of the invited audience received similar treatment when they expressed their views about Anglo-Irish political violence. One was Irishman Tom Durkin, as prominent member of Brent Trades Council and well-known throughout the labour movement.

Neither spoke in favour of republican or unionist paramilitaries, yet others who supported the use of political violence in Sri Lanka and South Africa were allowed to speak for themselves.

The Wilson document had more surprises:
'Irish rebel songs in genuine performances will be all right. In certain circumstances they could be restricted, for instance if sung by demonstrators. Consult.

How this interpretation is to be interpreted remains a puzzle. Does it mean that performers are not sincere about what they sing, but demonstrators are ? Or is it that audiences listen to the words of a crowd, but not those of the professional singer?

Paul McCartney's song 'Give Ireland back to the Irish' was banned in 1972. Since October 1988 songs performed by the Dubliners ('Kelly the boy from Killane'), Christy Moore ('Unfinished Revolution'), and The Pogues ('Streets of Sorrow/Birmingham Six') have all been hit by the Broadcasting Ban. However, the IBA admitted that it would not ban 'The Soldiers Song' - the Irish national anthem, most often sung by crowds. It contains sentiments which some elements in the British Government might consider inflammatory if they understood Irish.

The first victims

On the evening of 19 October 1988 the BBC and ITN re-ran footage from a lunchtime Sinn Fein press conference pointing out that the voices of those speaking could no longer be broadcast.

During the week the Ban was introduced, members of the Derry Film & Video Collective were in London for discussion with Channel 4 about the final form of their film about women in the republican tradition.

'*Mother Ireland*' had excited commissioning editors at C4 because it contained an interview with Mairead Farrell, the IRA volunteer shot dead by the SAS in Gibraltar. There had been protracted negotiations about many elements of the film, but it now became the first documentary to be axed under the Ban.

Although it went on to win awards in Europe in its uncut form, C4 would only show an edited version during a 1991 season of banned material.

Soon after the Ban was introduced an internal BBC memo warned regional reporters:
'It has already become clear that it is the Government's intention to stop us carrying actuality of figures such as Ken Livingstone or Senator Edward Kennedy should they express direct support for any of the named organisations'.

Broadcasters are under a legal, and moral, obligation to present news and information dispassionately. The most obvious way to ensure that the public knows when news is being censored is to issue 'health warnings'.

Reports from South Africa frequently contained 'sub-titles' or voice-overs' to indicate that they had been prepared 'under restrictions' imposed by an external agency.

For a while fairly straightforward 'disclaimers' were attached to items that were affected by the Ban. Methods of alerting the public to the new constraints have since become more sophisticated and imaginative - including the use of actors with more or less appropriate accents to dub over words used by banned persons 'in sync' with their lips.

Such editorial niceties are costly and time-consuming, and broadcast news works to tight deadlines. Even if this had not entered into the Government's original calculation, the simplest way to avoid such tiresome tokenism is to drop items which might require doctoring, or rely entirely on a reporter's words and the opinions of 'safe' experts.

Under the circumstances self-censorship, whether conscious or otherwise, becomes inevitable.

Institutionalised censorship

Five years on, in 1993, interpretations of the Ban have been codified in new guidelines issued by the broadcasting authorities.

The BBC speaks for them all with an admission in its current advice to staff that coverage of Ireland is a 'legal and political minefield' and suggests that editors should always seek advice from its Solicitors Department.

Specifically on the Ban, BBC producers are warned:
'If for example, a United States Senator spoke in the Senate or any other American context in support of Sinn Fein, a voice recording of his comments could not be used in our programmes.

And:
'The same applies to an MP speaking outside the House of Commons.
'It applies to ordinary members of the public.'

But:
'TV could show pictures of say UDA demonstrators waving banners of support for the UDA. The sound would have to be cut if they chanted support for the UDA.'

There is a rider, which appears to make a nonsense of the application of the ban to Bernadette McAliskey and others in the *Nation* programme:
'Generalised comments about or even in favour of terrorism in Ireland or about Irish republicanism are not prevented.'

Where the ban does apply, the need for 'health warnings' is emphasised. 'When a programme or programme item is materially changed in accordance with the Notice it is right to alert the audience to the fact. The words used should be clear and as specific as possible about the nature of the change.'

The section ends:
'When something is not in conflict with the Home Secretary's Notice the normal process of referral must still be followed.'

BBC programme-makers handling Irish stories are told to contact, in the first instance, the Head of News & Current Affairs NI who may, together with the appropriate News & Current Affairs Editor, refer the matter to the Director of News & Current Affairs and inform the Controller of Editorial Policy.

'It is very important that the BBC in Belfast is kept aware of the evolution of projects, including the inevitable changes which take place as ideas are developed.'

'...consultation must extend to production and transmission dates.'

These rules also apply to items appearing in BBC publications, promotional and publicity material.

The BBC denies that its Northern Ireland staff have a power of veto, but all items 'touching on Ireland in general or on Northern Ireland in particular' must be referred to the Controller NI, with any disagreements referred to the Deputy Director General of the BBC.

Criminalising journalism

Broadcasting staff are warned that since the Criminal Law Act (NI) 1967 and the Prevention of Terrorism Act (Temporary Provisions Act) 1976, journalists, as citizens are obliged :

'to provide information (to the police) about, and refrain from dealing with, criminals or terrorists in Northern Ireland.

'The NI (Emergency Provisions) Acts could also have an important bearing on programme makers'.

As the ITC and Radio Authority guidelines point out, unlike the position in English law, conviction for withholding information under the Criminal Law Act (NI) 1967 does not require proof that someone has misled or actively assisted a criminal.

The ITC's Programme Code dated February 1991 offers another exemplary warning :

'An interview conducted in Northern Ireland with a hooded person or the contriving by a production team of an incident involving hooded persons could be a breach of the NI (Emergency Provisions) (Amendment) Act 1975. It is not an offence to show film or pictures of persons wearing hoods so long as it is clear that the incident was not 'set up' in collusion with those wearing hoods. In practice, crews are likely to be invited to attend 'something of interest', usually a volley of shots or a show of arms by men in hoods.

'Film of such incidents should not be included in a programme without prior reference to the licensee's most senior programme executive or the designated alternate. *(Their emphasis)*

To avoid embarrassment all round, a comfortable British compromise now ensures that sensitive issues are avoided or routinely pushed onto the back burner.

Trying to gain interest let alone finance for independent TV productions treating of controversial topics like Ireland is more difficult than ever. In shame-faced self-justification editors and producers will shrug 'Who wants to know about Northern Ireland anyway ?'.

A few brave attempts at imaginative re-interpretation of the Ban will no doubt be made during 1994, the twenty-fifth anniversary of the deployment of British troops on the streets of the North of Ireland.

However the Ban has done little to dissuade either republican or unionist paramilitaries from the belief that they can bomb and shoot their way onto the TV screens.

Any continuation of violence merely justifies further repressive measures and hinders genuine opportunities for political progress. Meanwhile both the British and Irish people are expected to make do with whatever material their governments want them to receive.

If they are appalled and sick of 'The Troubles' it is through enforced ignorance and lack of any substantial information on which to base an informed opinion.

7. Opposition to the Ban

The Chair of the BBC Board of Governors Marmaduke Hussey called the Ban "a damaging precedent" that would make "reporting of Northern Ireland affairs incomplete", but the IBA issued a mealy-mouthed statement "welcoming the opportunity that parliament will have for a full debate at an early date and will be urging the Home Secretary to keep this policy under review".

Tory MP Cyril Townsend was more forthright in his criticism of the government's action :

> "I bet that in the United States people were outraged by the broadcasts about Vietnam. They would rather not have seen what was happening in Vietnam. But who in the House (of Commons) could get up and say how wrong it was that the citizens of the United State were outraged by what they saw in Vietnam? People had to face facts and certain political consequences flowed from that."

Many Labour and Liberal/Democrat MPs voiced their alarm and anger about the Ban and have remained implacably opposed to it. Former SDLP MP Lord Fitt and Lord (Roy) Mason, a former Labour NI Minister, thought it should have gone further.

The most consistent opposition to the Ban has come from the media unions, from press freedom and civil liberties groups like the CPBF, Article 19 and Liberty (NCCL).

> *As soon as the Ban was announced, the NUJ tested the feelings of its members in broadcasting about the possibility of protest action.*
> *At first the union was confident of support for a day of action on Thurs 10 November 1988, "to protest at the assault on freedom of speech and the public's right to know".*
> *BBC World Service staff were particularly incensed, believing that the Ban called into question their reputation for even-handed coverage of difficult issues elsewhere in the world. They voted 6:1 in favour of a strike action.*

BBC journalists in Belfast issued a strong statement condemning the Ban as 'an attack on free speech and information', and pointing out that broadcasters were being discriminated against while their colleagues on newspapers had a freer hand to provide 'fair and balanced coverage'.

The NUJ acknowledged the special difficulties of broadcast journalists in the North of Ireland and did not expect them to join in a strike. After initial reticence members there decided to take part to ensure a united front. Everyone had in mind the impact of the united action by broadcasters in both public and commercial sectors over the 'Real Lives' ban in 1985.

On that occasion the then Home Secretary Leon Brittan had leaned on the BBC Governors after Mrs Thatcher expressed her anger to a Sunday Times journalist having been told that a leading republican was to feature in a BBC documentary called 'At the Edge of the Union'.
A one-day national strike resulted in a climbdown by the BBC Governors and senior management, and the eventual broadcast of a slightly modified version of the programmes.

The new Employment Act of 1988 required comprehensive balloting and advance notice to employers if a strike was to be legal.
The NUJ contacted senior management at the BBC and ITN where a 'Yes' vote was crucial. At the BBC John Birt, then Deputy Director General, caused uncertainty by trying to persuade staff that a strike would be hitting at the Corporation rather than the Government. At ITN the strike vote was lost.
These setbacks, and assurances from BBC and commercial broadcasting executives of a vigorous campaign of joint opposition led the NUJ General Secretary to call off the industrial action at short notice.

Instead some journalists lobbied their MPs and attended a meeting in Parliament where for the first and, so far, the last time senior TV executives shared a platform of opposition to the Ban alongside media union General Secretaries and an all-Party panel of MPs.

There was some bitterness among the NUJ membership at the missed opportunity, especially in the provinces where the principle had been argued over and won at a difficult time. Many felt, correctly, that management promises of vigorous action would not materialise.

Commemorating the ban

In 1989 the first anniversary was marked with a series of well-co-ordinated events. About 1,000 people took part in the first of several annual marches organised by the NUJ.

They were led by media union General Secretaries wearing gags who delivered protests to the headquarters of BBC, Independent TV News and Channel 4 in central London.

NUJ members at the BBC's 'listening post' in Caversham announced: 'From the unique position of monitoring foreign broadcasts which are in many cases determined or limited by state or party policy, members of this chapel express their concern about moves which are a limitation of the freedom of expression within the broadcasting media. These moves are felt to be prejudicial to unbiased coverage of opinion and to be an unwelcome historical precedent'.

A rally featuring media, political and show-business opponents of the Ban was held at the Dominion Theatre, followed by a lobby of Parliament.

Broadcasters devoted special programmes and items to considering the implications of the Ban, and in Britain's media centres journalists and others held public meetings and token pickets.

The CPBF and Information on Ireland delivered a petition containing 5,000 signatures of media workers and public figures from around the world, calling on the Government to lift the Ban.

By convenient coincidence the judiciary helped the Government to side-step the embarrassment of such hostile attention by choosing 19 October 1989 to release the innocent Guildford Four. Cameras turned from Irish protestors against the ban who had chained themselves to the railings of the Palace of Westminster to follow the arrival of Paul Hill and Gerry Conlon at a hastily-called press conference in the very room where a protest meeting against the Ban was being held.

That night the world's media relayed the jubilant scenes outside the Old Bailey as Gerry Conlon punched the air with delight. At a crucial moment the apparent magnanimity of the British authorities obscured its culpability.

Two days later the IBA instructed Channel 4 to drop a live *After Dark* discussion programme on censorship featuring Sinn Fein MP Gerry Adams. C4 complied.

Two months after delivering its petition, the CPBF received a response from the Government repeating past justifications and offering an assurance that the ban would remain "under review"

'..it is simply not acceptable for the public platform of TV and radio to be used (by those now banned) in a way that causes offence to the vast majority of people and on occasion to threaten and intimidate law-abiding citizens.'

The restrictions did not (*pace* Mrs Thatcher)

'represent a serious diminution of civil liberties. They are limited measure aimed at a specific source of harm'.

The reply claimed that

'terrorists and their apologists have taken advantage of these opportunities (to broadcast) to exploit and manipulate the media.'

The ban, it said, had closed off

'a major avenue of propaganda, with beneficial results to the whole of the United Kingdom. The public are well aware of what the terrorists and their apologists stand for'.

In 1990 the media unions, the CPBF and other anti-censorship groups, set up *Time to Know*, an ad-hoc campaign to focus attention on the Ban, but the second anniversary demonstration was less well-attended. Radical changes in broadcasting law and industrial relations had by now switched the attention of media workers to more 'bread and butter' concerns.

Protest action in 1991 included an NUJ/CPBF day conference which broadened the issue to include other aspects of censorship and freedom of information.

By 1992 letters of protest in the national press were the most public expressions of continued objections to the Ban.

Legal action

It has been left to the NUJ, backed by the broadcast technicians' union BECTU and Article 19, to challenge the Ban in the courts.

Six NUJ members lodged their objections in December 1988. Their case in favour of the right to know was rejected by the British courts and the House of Lords the following year.

As the fifth anniversary of the Ban approaches the NUJ is awaiting a decision of the European Commission on Human Rights as to whether the British Government should appear before the European Court.

Despite worthy sentiments of antipathy to the Ban from senior broadcasting executives like John Birt and Liz Forgan, not one British broadcasting company has been willing even to contribute to the costs, let alone join forces in the NUJ's action.

In 1992 BBC chiefs were invited by the media unions to participate in a protest delegation to Heritage Secretary and former NI Minister Peter Brooke. They turned down this latest opportunity to live up to the commitment made to the NUJ in 1988.

8. Living with the ban

In Britain attention has focused on the civil liberties issues raised by the ban, and interest has faltered as its effects further sanitised coverage from across the Irish Sea.

In the North of Ireland the impact of the ban was quite different. John Conway, the BBC's head of News & Current Affairs in Belfast described in the Corporation's house journal what it meant for his staff .

> 'The perception has grown up that we can still interview Sinn Fein about the state of the roads, blocked drains or other innocuous local issues. Not so. Every broadcast interview with a member of the party has to go through a much finer filter and that's what becomes so time consuming for editors and their journalists,...
> 'To ensure that an interview with (a) councillor could be broadcast, the news editor at Radio Foyle (in Derry) had to check with me in Belfast and I, in turn, had to consult, with senior colleagues in London about potential legal and policy implications before the green light to broadcast was given. All that for the everyday voice of grassroots politics which local radio is there to articulate.' *(Aerial 24/1/89)*

Conway was eventually transferred from Belfast after threats against his life were made by the IRA.

At an anti-censorship conference organised by the *Andersonstown News* in the wake of the Ban, members of the nationalist community in West Belfast applauded Irish journalist Nell McCafferty, who had suffered professional ostracism after admitting sympathy for the IRA, when she urged people to "cuddle a journalist".

The audience acknowledged that journalists are one of their few hopes for alerting the world to the discrimination and alienation they suffer.

Despite being the most evident target of the Ban, Sinn Fein has also repudiated the intimidation of journalists, preferring to supply information whether or not it would be used.

According to its then Director of Publicity Danny Morrison, in the four

30

months prior to the Ban the Republican Press Centre in Belfast received 417 enquiries from British broadcasters. In the four months afterwards there were only 110 such calls.

A study by Glasgow University Media Group, published in 1990, revealed that Sinn Fein members were seen or heard on British network TV news on 93 occasions in the year before the ban but only 34 times in the following year (a drop of 63%).

To counter the impact of the Ban, Sinn Fein increased the range of local bulletins it distributed, but plans for pirate radio stations and video-newsletters were quietly abandoned.

News without the quotes

In the the North of Ireland daily news bulletins, current affairs programmes and live debates and phone-ins can hardly avoid dealing with spokespeople for banned organisations or those likely to support them, if they are to reflect what is happening on the streets.

Whether they talk to people who are covered by the Ban or avoid them, journalists are bound to face taunts from politicians and members of both communities just for trying to do their job.

Soon after the Ban was introduced journalists covering a republican march through West Belfast found themselves checking with people inside the compound at the Sinn Fein headquarters whether they were a member or supporter of the party before recording them.

Colleagues from Radio Telefis Eireann (RTE, the Irish broadcasting service), who are subject to similar restrictions under Section 31 of the Irish Broadcasting Act, explained that one way of 'covering your back' is to record on tape a brief question and answer about whether or not a potential interviewee is a member or supporter of a proscribed organisation. If they say they are not, then an interview can be recorded for broadcast.

One reporter said that the best thing to do was to assume that anyone in nationalist strongholds like West Belfast or Derry is likely to have republican sympathies, and those in the Protestant areas were likely to sympathise with Loyalist paramilitaries - so the best thing to do was to rely on public figures who were known to be 'safe'.

Since the Ban came into effect, the Social Democratic and Labour Party (SDLP), has taken the West Belfast parliamentary seat from Gerry Adams. Even before he became the new MP, the SDLP candidate Dr Joe Hendron, was regularly interviewed by broadcasters about local issues. His party represents a nationalist viewpoint which is not covered by the Ban.

In the autumn of 1988, just after Thatcher's August Security Review
Conference the RUC carried out a lengthy series of raids on republican
and loyalist residential areas throughout the North. Single houses and
whole streets were being sealed off for up to 30 hours at a time. Some
homes were then ripped apart in a search for weapons.
Relatively few weapons were found, although in some cases pneumatic
drills were taken to concrete floors leaving massive craters in the
kitchens of innocent householders. Where nothing was found distraught
families were simply told to apply for compensation.
The operation, said to have been aimed at 1,000 homes by Christmas
1988, received little media coverage.
The clear implication of the raids was that those whose homes were
searched had something to hide, including a supposed connection with
a proscribed organisation.
It was a chilling illustration of the impcat of the Ban. In West Belfast the
likelihood was that the victims would be represented by Sinn Fein
councillors or Gerry Adams MP, now effectively silenced in the confusion
over how the Ban was supposed to work.

The ironies of the situation extend far beyond the vested interests of either nationalist or unionist communities.

The exigencies of the Ban forced TV news agency Visnews (now Reuters TV) to make two versions of material filmed in the North of Ireland for supply to broadcasters. The one for British terrestrial channels has to acknowledge the constraints of the Ban, that for overseas consumption can ignore them.

One of its customers, Sky TV, which broadcasts on a satellite channel that transcends national borders, became the first company to be reprimanded for an apparent breach of the Ban in July 1990, after screeening an item from a Canadian news bulletin.

9. The Irish dimension

In the Republic of Ireland political censorship is as bad, if not worse than in Britain.

The British government claims that its measures merely echo those applied by the Irish Government under Section 31 of its Broadcasting Act.

The Minister for Post and Telecommunications has powers similar to those in British broadcasting legislation. They were first used in 1971 to stop the 'autonomous' state broadcasting service RTE from transmitting material "that could be calculated to promote the activities of any organisation" involved in or encouraging "the attainment of any particular objective by violent means".

When RTE broadcast an interview with the IRA Chief of Staff in November 1972, the entire RTE Board of Government appointees was sacked, and journalist Kevin Kelly was jailed for three months.

In 1976 the Dail (Irish parliament) approved an amendment to Section 31 devised by erstwhile journalist and diplomat Conor Cruise O'Brien, then the Minister responsible in the Fine Gael/Labour coalition government.

In effect it allowed the British government to determine who should be allowed to speak on Irish airwaves, since the organisations banned under the amendment were those proscribed by Britain in the North of Ireland, plus Sinn Fein - a legal political party which was then rebuilding electoral support in the Republic.

Ironically British broadcasts can be received in Ireland, so viewers and listeners could still see or hear the forbidden broadcasts by tuning into services which were then not subject to such restrictions.

Any appearance on RTE by *known* Sinn Fein members speaking about *anything* is anathema - one 'Sinner' who confessed his membership was stopped from discussing mushrooms on an RTE gardening 'phone-in.

Only months before the Hurd ban came into effect a young RTE radio reporter, Jennie McGeever, was sacked for including the voices of two prominent Sinn Fein members in a tape broadcast only hours after she had completed an overnight assignment accompanying the bodies of the Gibraltar victims from Dublin to the north. Gerry Adams and Martin McGuiness were calming the crowd and the police during a tense moment on the funeral cortege; the tape was pulled after only a few of their words had been broadcast.

McGeever's editors, who would normally take responsibility for the broadcast item remained in post, and she had to take legal action to win compensation.

Fresh challenges

In 1990 RTE refused to broadcast interviews about a major industrial dispute with Bakers' Union official, Larry O'Toole, a Sinn Fein member. Even after the success of his legal action against the state broadcaster in July 1992, RTE still refused to carry an interview with O'Toole.

RTE's 'over-scrupulous' interpretation of Section 31 has been presented both as a way of protesting against censorship and as a way of avoiding trouble with nervous governments.

The British Government smugly reminds opponents of its own version that similar restrictions had been operating in Ireland for 12 years - as if one form of censorship justifies another.

An attempt to persuade the European Courts that Section 31 violates human rights in Ireland has failed, but in January 1993 Irish journalists, backed by the NUJ and Ireland's largest union SIPTU, launched a high-profile 'Let in the Light' campaign to press for greater freedom of expression in the Republic.

In the summer of 1993 the United Nations Committee on the International Covenant on Civil & Political Rights (ICCPR) ruled that Section 31 is a definite breach of Article 19 of the Covenant. It will be interesting to see how both the Irish and British governments respond.

Britain has derogated from those articles of the ICCPR which oblige states to produce detainees before a judicial authority within 48 hours - because it runs counter to the purpose of the Prevention of Terrorism Act. And it has yet to ratify two of the Optional Protocols which allow citizens a direct right of appeal to the UN and outlaw the death penalty in peacetime.

Seventy years ago partition was enforced, under threat of war, against the consent of the vast majority of Irish people after two general elections had given Sinn Fein enormous all-Ireland majorities in favour of a united, independent republic. For some years now opinion polls conducted in Britain have shown that the majority of British people want British troops out of Ireland.

Section 31 and the British Broadcasting Ban have been presented as buttresses for democracy. Unlike its Irish equivalent, the strictures of the British Ban are lifted during elections.

However, few British or Irish politicians would accept that they were operating in a free democracy if the only time they were allowed to broadcast direct to the electorate was in the few weeks before voting took place. And if they were denied access to the airwaves as soon as their victory had been declared.

CPBF National Secretary Tom O'Malley puts the organisations arguments against the ban at a protest rally.

10. The international dimension

Among those who have delivered protests about the Ban are the International Federation of Journalists, the Belgian journalists' union and FAIR (Fairness and Accuracy in Reporting), the CPBF's sister organisation in the USA.

But it is not just journalists who have expressed concern about the implications of the broadcasting 'restrictions'.

Emigration has created huge Irish communities throughout the English-speaking world and the repercussions of this convoluted form of censorship have been felt where ever a country relies upon British sources for information about Ireland.

A few of the ancestors of the Irish abroad were forced to leave Ireland because of their political or military involvement in the struggle for independence. Many more left as a direct result of the impact of British Government policies on the Irish economy - from the artificial famines of the nineteenth century to the effects of the trade war between Britain and Ireland which lasted from the 1930s to the 1950s.

At the time of partition in 1921 Britain had demanded reparations of the Irish Free State. In response, Eamonn de Valera refused to pay rents to British absentee landlords when he became Taoiseach (Prime Minister) in 1934. Britain's reaction was to boycott Irish goods, causing fresh hardship to the emergent Republic.

Whatever their political persuasion, many of the millions of people of Irish descent worldwide hope that international pressure, or even the intervention of the United Nations, might eventually bring about a political solution to the centuries-old conflict between Britain and Ireland.

Soon after the Ban was introduced a group of concerned Australians contacted the CPBF to draw attention to the far-reaching impact of the new and existing restrictions on coverage of Ireland in the British media.

'No Australian media organisation has a reporter based in Northern

36

Ireland. Many have London-based correspondents, who may occasionally cover an Irish story.

'The vast bulk of reports used (in Australia) are taken from British-based wire services, British newspaper reports, BBC-TV and ITV and BBC radio. This in itself is a problem, as these reports are made in a British context and tend to reflect Britain's particular relationship with Ireland.

'Since (the ban) Australian TV and radio has continued to carry material from British sources. Without public discussion or knowledge, the Australian media coverage of events and issues in Northern Ireland is now subjected to censorship..'

And in the summer of 1993, the American Corporation for Public Broadcasting (CPB) found itself under siege from the Irish National Caucus for continuing to transmit BBC material about the north of Ireland without a 'health warning'. Some Irish Americans are demanding that the CPB should stop buying any material from the BBC.

James Mullin of the Irish American Unity Confernece, who initiated the campaign explains:

'My major concern is that the CPB, which was created to prevent government interference and control, is allowing state-controlled news to be broadcast over the public airwaves; not only allowing it, but underwriting it to the tune of $100,000 of our tax dollars last year.'

An energetic campaign has now been mounted in Washington to persuade members of the Senate to withhold funding to the CPB unless and until 'health warnings' are broadcast alongside any BBC material.

The British Government has always been anxious about the power of the Irish lobby in the United States, and has put a great deal of effort into countering what it regards as the false impressions given by 'irresponsible' media coverage. Witness its efforts to counter the success of the campaign for the adoption of the MacBride (anti-discrimination) Principles by US-companies investing in the North of Ireland, and its efforts to persuade President Clinton to rethink his plans for a peace envoy.

37

11. A shameful anniversary

October 19 is a shameful anniversary. It is a reminder of the acquiescence of the broadcasting establishment who delude themselves that their function is to examine and challenge the activities of institutions and individuals who hold power in society.

It is a reminder that the British Government prefers to stifle open debate and ignore the wishes of the majority of the British electorate that British troops should get out of Ireland.

It is a reminder to journalists and civil libertarians that any concession to political censorship weakens us all.

Whatever token protests are made on the anniversary itself, the British and Irish people have a right to know what is being done in their name and how it affects the lives of others.

When lives are being lost, and vast sums of public money spent on 'security', every voter in Britain deserves to know why. And that includes being able to hear every shade of opinion in the North of Ireland.

The media in thrall

Britain's proud boast to be the home of freedom and democracy rings hollow for all sections of the community in the North of Ireland, and for those who may yet die because censorship of the media has reduced the chance of full public debate about the causes and opportunities for resolution of the conflict.

Journalists are unable to function there in the way they manage to in war zones further afield, where Britain is not directly involved

The partition of Ireland has lasted longer than Soviet communism, longer than the Berlin Wall and the-stand off between the PLO and state of Israel, and longer than institutionalised *apartheid* in South Africa.

Despite censorship, the media supplied many vivid images and accounts of those apparently intractable problems and helped to mould international opinion against the injustices they represented.

38

Yet on Britain's doorstep, in its last and oldest colony, the media can only tell that part of the story which the British Government will allow. Broadcast journalists are expected to adopt a standpoint defined by an artificial all-Party consensus constructed over the last 25 years to defend the policies of whichever Government is in power.

Controversy about media management by the military and political authorities during the Falklands conflict and the Gulf War has highlighted the extent to which hideous events can be sanitised when journalists are hog-tied. Those who dare to sidestep the censors, refuse to take sides or offer criticism lay themselves open to the taunt - 'If you are not with us you are against us.'

By placing the onus on broadcasters to apply the Ban, the Government has encouraged self-censorship and blunted the spirit of enquiry that motivates most journalists. Once journalists get into the bad habit of avoiding controversy rather than seeking it out, the damage has been done to independent inquiry. And that is inimical to democracy.

Busting the ban

In Greece, when the editor of Eleftherotypia was arrested under the criminal code in 1991, for publishing a statement by the November 19 terror group, six other editors immediately published the same statement in solidarity and were jailed. Their incarceration lasted 10 days. The Government climbed down, agreeing to reconsider the application of the law as it related to the Press.
And in the summer of 1993 the Greek Government fell apart after a series of bugging scandals and attempts to muzzle the media which had grown bolder in its exposure of corruption.

What would, or could, any British Government do if all Britain's broadcasting companies refused to comply with the Home Secretary's executive order ?

It could remove broadcasting licences; it might take legal action and fine, or jail, senior broadcasting executives; it might even place all broadcasting under direct state control. But would it?

No British government would risk such action if it wanted to stay in office. For all its sabre-rattling about the excesses of the tabloid Press, the current British government has backed away from any attempt to curb the Press in the face of united opposition from national, regional and local newspaper editors.

Its constitutional relationship with the broadcast media is very different.

39

Government plans for the future of broadcasting already had chief executives, and broadcasters further down the chain of command, squirming with anxiety at the time the ban was introduced.

The catalogue of programmes tampered with or taken off the airwaves over the last 34 years is evidence enough that Ireland is seldom an issue for which the broadcasting establishment is prepared to go to the wall.

With the *sang froid* of Pontius Pilate the Government maintains that it is up to the broadcasting authorities to uphold the law and take appropriate action if anyone breaches the rules.

"The Government simply does not envisage a situation where the BBC Board of Governors or the ITC would allow the rules to be broken," says the DNH with perhaps justifiable confidence, adding for good measure: "It is not for the Government to get involved in the day-to-day issues of broadcasting."

The Independent Television Commission which now regulates British commercial TV admits that it has made no formal representation to government about the restrictions. However it has not been backward at raising other pressing commercial and legislative issues with the Minister on behalf of the broadcasters.

"We have always supported the flexible and creative interpretation of the ban, particularly by C4," explains a spokesperson, indicating that if the Government wanted to do anything about broadcasters who "push interpretation to the outer limits of acceptability" it would be up to the Government to take action themselves.

Only a flagrant or persistent breach of a broadcaster's license agreement, which includes the ITC Programme Codes, would result in direct action by the Commission. Under the Broadcasting Act 1990 it is empowered to warn, fine (up to 5% of a company's net advertising revenue), and shorten or eventually revoke a broadcaster's licence for breaching the regulations.

In practice the ITC has preferred to let sleeping dogs lie, and is unsure what action it could or would take if all the broadcasters breached the ban.

Perhaps the last word could be left to the one person most directly targeted by the 'restrictions', Sinn Fein's Gerry Adams.

He is not alone in believing that the best way for British broadcasters to tackle state censorship is also the simplest: "Bust the ban."

FURTHER READING

BBC PRODUCERS GUIDELINES
Available from BBC

ITC PROGRAMME CODES
Available from ITC

RADIO AUTHORITY PROGRAMME
CODES Available from RA

TELEVISING TERRORISM : Political
violence in popular culture
Eds. Schlesinger, Murdock & Elliot
Comedia 1983

IRELAND : THE PROPAGANDA WAR
Liz Curtis Pluto Press 1984

THE MOST CONTRARY REGION: The
BBC in Northern Ireland
Rex Cathcart Blackstaff 1984

NOTHING BUT THE SAME OLD STORY:
The roots of anti-Irish racism
Liz Curtis Information on Ireland, 1984

CENSORING 'THE TROUBLES': an Irish
solution to an Irish problem
IFJ, 1987

THE HURD BROADCASTING BAN :
Synopsis of press coverage
Mike Jempson NUJ/CPBF 1988

THE WINDLESHAM/RAMPTON REPORT
ON 'DEATH ON THE ROCK'
Lord Windlesham & Richard Rampton
QC Faber & Faber 1989

IRELAND: THE CENSORED SUBJECT
Danny Morrison Sinn Fein 1989

NO COMMENT : Censorship, Secrecy
and the Irish Troubles
Article 19 1989

PRESS FREEDOM UNDER ATTACK IN
BRITAIN
Mia Doornaert & Sven Egil Omdal IFJ,
1989

WHO FRAMED COLIN WALLACE ?
Paul Foot MacMillan 1989

WAR WITHOUT HONOUR
Fred Holroyd Medium 1989

DEATH ON THE ROCK and other stories
Roger Bolton WH Allen/Optimum 1990

SPEAK NO EVIL: The British
Broadcasting Ban, the Media & the
Conflict in Ireland
Henderson/Miller/Reilly Glasgow
University Media Group, 1990,

THE MEDIA & NORTHERN IRELAND:
Covering the Troubles
Ed. Bill Rolston MacMillan 1991

MEDIA STATE AND NATION: Political
violence and collective identities
Philip Schlesinger Sage 1991

THE STALKER AFFAIR & THE PRESS
David Murphy Unwin Hyman 1991

GETTING THE MESSAGE
Glasgow University Media Group
Routledge 1993

HUMAN RIGHTS AND THE UNITED
KINGDOM: The Challenge to Government
Ed. Mike Jempson Crantock/AI 1993

Some of these titles are available through the
CPBF Mail Order Catalogue, available from
CPBF, 8 Cynthia Street, London N1 9JF   Tel: 071 278 4430

A CATALOGUE OF CENSORSHIP 1959-1993

by Liz Curtis

The list of programmes from 1959 to October 1983 was published in *Ireland: the Propaganda War* (Pluto, 1984) and Liz Curtis drew partly on the chronology by Paul Madden in *The British Media and Ireland: Truth the First Casualty* (Information on Ireland, 1979) to compile it.

The listings since 1983 have been compiled by Liz Curtis for Information on Ireland briefings. They include some items which were important but did not involve censorship and these are indicated by **

Before the Ban

1959 - BBC
SEE IT NOW (Ed Murrow talk show)
  Lord Brookeborough, then Prime Minister of Northern Ireland, personally intervened to secure the dropping of the second of two interviews with actress Siobhan McKenna. He did this because she had, in the first interview, referred to IRA internees in the Republic as 'young idealists'.

1959 - BBC
TONIGHT
  Seven 10-minute reports by Alan Whicker about the Six Counties were dropped after the personal intervention of Lord Brookeborough. Eight reports were planned, but only the first was transmitted: its subject was betting shops, but passing references to the political situation led to a major row and the banning of the succeeding reports.

July 1966 - ITV
THIS WEEK
  A programme which depicted Ian Paisley as a tub-thumping bible basher was not allowed to be shown in the North of Ireland.

June 1968 - BBC
  The BBC refused to do a feature programme about Austin Currie's protest occupation of a Dungannon council house which had been allocated to an unmarried Unionist. This became a *cause celebre* within the BBC.

1970 - BBC
The BBC commissioned Jim Allen to write a contemporary play about the North of Ireland, to be directed by Ken Loach and produced by Tony Garnett. The BBC stopped the project when the script was partially written. The play was about the politics of the Officials and the Provisionals. (Jim Allen went on to write a film script for Kestrel Films about the 1919-21 war against Britain, to be called *The Rising*; a Swedish company agreed to put up more than half the money providing some money could be raised in England, but no English company would finance it.)

July 1970 - BBC
PANORAMA
The programme included interviews with relatives of six people killed in Belfast. BBC Northern Ireland 'opted out' on the grounds that the programme was inflammatory. This was the first such 'opting out'. (BBC policy was that programmes should be identical in Britain and the North of Ireland.)

February 1971 - BBC
24 HOURS
A film which showed widespread disenchantment among Unionists with Northern Ireland Prime Minister Major Chichester Clark. The film was delayed by BBC Northern Ireland Controller Waldo Maguire. When the predicted resignation took place, the film became superfluous and was never shown.

August 1971 - BBC
24 HOURS
Senior BBC executives prevented *24 Hours* from doing an in-depth programme about the IRA. The Chief Assistant to the Director-General, John Crawley, said, 'Such a programme setting out the roots of the IRA would not be acceptable.' (See *Private Eye*, 15 November 1971.)

October 1971 - BBC
The BBC filmed the proceedings of the Assembly of the Northern Irish People, which had been set up by the SDLP and the Nationalist Party as an alternative to the Stormont Parliament. The footage was never shown, possibly because it was deemed 'unbalanced' (*The Sunday Times*, 2 January 1972).

November 1971 - Granada
WORLD IN ACTION: 'South of the Border'
Granada wanted to do a programme showing how the 'troubles' in the North were building up pressures in the South of Ireland. The film included Sean MacStiofain (Provisional IRA Chief of Staff) and Ruairi O Bradaigh

(Provisional Sinn Fein President), and also Dublin politicians who were hostile to the IRA. The Independent Television Authority banned the programme before it was completed. ITA Chairman Lord Aylestone felt it was 'aiding and abetting the enemy'. Granada went ahead and completed the programme, but, on viewing it, the ITA confirmed the ban.

1971 - ITN
ITN suppressed a film about an army post surrounding a lone policeman on the Creggan estate in Derry.

November 1971 - BBC
24 HOURS
The BBC filmed a number of statements by ex-internees about their treatment at the hands of the British army during detention. Despite the mounting evidence of the torture carried in the press, the BBC delayed screening the films until after the publication of the Compton Report. The films were balanced by a discussion between a Tory MP, Anthony Buck, and former Labour Defence Minister, Roy Hattersley.

February 1972 - Thames
THIS WEEK: 'Aftermath of Bloody Sunday'
(also titled, 'Bloody Sunday - Two Sides of the Story')
Thames was preparing a programme piecing together, through interviews with witnesses and soldiers, the story of Bloody Sunday, when paratroopers shot dead 13 civilians in Derry. With the announcement of the Widgery inquiry, 10 Downing Street sought a blanket ban on media coverage. Thames compromised by showing a complete unedited roll of an interview with a Welsh ex-warrant officer, who lived in the area, balanced by a complete roll of accounts by Scottish paratroopers (one of whom, a lieutenant, later admitted to the Widgery Tribunal that his statement in the film that he had seen a gunman, was a lie). Twenty rolls of film, including interviews with Catholic Bogsiders, were never used: these contained more damaging material.

August 1972 - BBC
PANORAMA: 'Operation Motorman'
A Panorama team went into Creggan Heights in Derry alongside the Coldstream Guards during Operation Motorman, 31 July 1982, when the British army stormed the no-go areas in the city, dismantling the barricades put up by nationalist residents. Later that day the team - with reporter Alan Hart and producer Bill Cran - interviewed local people about their reactions. The film was suppressed on the orders of a senior BBC executive.

October 1972 - BBC
PLAY FOR TODAY: 'Carson Country'
This play by Dominic Behan was postponed from May, and finally transmitted on 23 October, 'to avoid provoking possible trouble during the marching season' (*Evening Standard*, 11 May 1972). The postponement was decided on by David Attenborough, Controller of TV programmes, and Northern Ireland Controller Waldo Maguire. The play was about 'the origin of the Stormont state'.

October 1972 - Thames
ARMCHAIR THEATRE: 'The Folk Singer'
The IBA asked to view this play by Dominic Behan, about a Liverpool folk singer who visits Belfast, before its proposed transmission date on 7 November. The IBA granted permission, but Thames chose to transmit it at 10.30 pm, instead of in *Armchair Theatre*'s usual nine o'clock slot.

November 1972 - BBC
A SENSE OF LOSS
The BBC refused to screen this film by Marcel Ophuls on the grounds that it was 'too pro-Irish' (*The Sunday Times*, 5 November 1972). The BBC had a financial involvement in the film, following their screening of Ophuls' *The Sorrow and the Pity*, which was much acclaimed. The film consisted of interviews with ordinary Protestants and Catholics as well as politicians and soldiers. The film was, by implication, critical of the Unionist case, and was also against violence from any quarter.

February 1973 - ATV
HANG UP YOUR BRIGHTEST COLOURS:
The Life and Death of Michael Collins
Following the success of Kenneth Griffith's BBC film on Cecil Rhodes, ATV commissioned him to make a historical documentary in the same vivid story-telling style. Griffith chose as his subject Michael Collins, IRA leader in the war against Britain in 1920 and a signatory of the treaty which led to civil war. A deeply committed film, possibly the best Griffith has ever made, it examines a crucial period of Irish history and condemns Britain's role. Sir Lew Grade, ATV's Managing Director, banned the film. It has never been shown, and even Kenneth Griffith does not have access to it.

March 1974 - BBC
CHILDREN IN CROSSFIRE
The Tory Northern Ireland Secretary tried to get this film stopped. BBC Northern Ireland Controller Dick Francis ordered major changes in the film.

45

Not satisfied with the changes made, he had its transmission stopped twic When it finally went out on 12 March, it had a one-minute announceme appended at the start implying that the government's Sunningdale policy h eased the tensions, depicted in the film, between the British army and peop in the republican areas of the North. The film's message was that childre there were growing up psychologically disturbed: this thesis was undermine by a follow-up film, *A Bright Brand New Day...?*, transmitted in Janua 1982 after a repeat of the first film.

November 1974 - Bristol Channel (Cable Television channel)
NEWSPEAK
On 29 November, when this local news programme had started, a ban can through from the Home Office on an interview with Adrian Gallagher, Sout West organiser of Clann na hEireann (the equivalent of Official Sinn Fein He was to discuss the Birmingham bombings. The Home Office regulate this and four other cable television experiments, and outline programm schedules had to be submitted to them at least two weeks in advance.

May 1975 - Thames
THIS WEEK: 'Hands Across the Sea'
This programme, about fund-raising for the IRA in America, was postpon for a week by the IBA. The programme was originally timed to be shown c the day of the elections for the Northern Ireland Convention, but would ha gone out half-an-hour after the polls had closed. The IBA postponed it becaus they said, 'the subject matter could have an unfortunate impact on opinio and emotions in the North of Ireland.

January 1976 - BBC
NATIONWIDE
On 8 January *Nationwide* showed a film on the SAS training, which had be on the shelf. Both negative and print were apparently later destroyed c 'advice' from the Ministry of Defence.

March 1976 - BBC
ARTICLE 5
A play commissioned by the BBC from Brian Phelan about three mercenarie torturers, who are commissioned by an Englishman to protect his interests an unspecified country. The message of the play, written with the assistan of Amnesty International, was against the use of torture: the North of Irela was mentioned in passing as an instance of the use of torture by government The play was recorded in January 1975 and banned by the BBC.

October 1976 - BBC Scotland
THE SCOTTISH CONNECTION
The BBC Northern Ireland Controller insisted that an interview with a Provisional IRA man be dropped from this film about the cultural and political links between Scotland and the North of Ireland. The cut was confirmed by Director-General Charles Curran. The producers intended to insert a statement saying that they could not show an interview with a Provisional IRA spokesman because it was against BBC policy, but that interviews with the legal Ulster Defence Association were permitted. This statement was omitted when the film was shown in Scotland on 23 October 1976 and on the network on 5 January 1977.

February 1977 - London Weekend
EIGHTEEN MONTHS TO BALCOMBE STREET
Shane Connaughton, the writer, asked for his name to be withdrawn from this reconstruction of the Balcombe Street siege because it had not been produced as he intended. 'I wanted to explain why the bombers were there,' he said (*The Irish Post*, 26 February 1977).

March 1977 - BBC
TONIGHT: Interview with Bernard O'Connor
Keith Kyle's interview with Bernard O'Connor, a Catholic school-teacher who alleged he had been ill-treated by the RUC at Castlereagh holding centre, was transmitted a week later than scheduled. The BBC governors thoroughly investigated the film before allowing transmission. In July 1980 O'Connor won £5,000 in compensation as exemplary damages for maltreatment. Both Roy Mason, then Northern Ireland Secretary, and Tory spokesperson Airey Neave condemned the BBC for showing the programme, and some newspapers blamed it for the killing of an RUC man by the IRA a few days later.

1977 - BBC
MAN ALIVE: 'A Street in Belfast' (also known as 'Short Strand')
The BBC commissioned this film from Eric Durschmied, a freelance film-maker, then refused to show it. The film focused on the daily lives of three families in the Short Strand, a small Catholic enclave in an overwhelmingly Protestant area of Belfast.

August 1977 - Thames
THIS WEEK: 'In Friendship and Forgiveness'
Peter Taylor, the reporter, described this film as 'an alternative diary' of the Queen's Jubilee visit to the North of Ireland. It challenged the pervasive media picture of a pacified province by showing that the visit had in fact heightened

the political divisions there. The IBA took exception to several sections of the film and banned it two minutes before transmission on 17 August. The film was eventually transmitted, with small alterations, two weeks after the visit, when its topicality was lost, at a variety of times in the various ITV regions.

October 1977 - Thames
THIS WEEK: 'Inhuman and Degrading Treatment'
This Week investigated 10 cases of alleged ill-treatment of people held by the RUC for interrogation. The IBA insisted that the RUC be represented, but the RUC refused to cooperate or to be interviewed. The Chief Constable offered, the day before transmission, a five-minute RUC statement to camera, which would not allow the reporter to question him. *This Week* was forced to accept this, because otherwise the IBA would not have allowed the programme to be shown.

February 1978 - Thames
THE GREEN, THE ORANGE AND THE RED, WHITE AND BLUE
David Elstein, *This Week* producer, and Peter Taylor, *This Week* reporter, offered Thames a historical project on the North of Ireland which would have mixed documentary with dramatised reconstruction. Thames refused the project, probably because Elstein and Taylor had previously been involved in controversy, and it might have once again brought Thames into conflict with the IBA. Elstein offered it to the BBC, who also turned it down.

May 1978 - London Weekend
WEEKEND WORLD
Soon after *Weekend World* started making this film assessing the current strength of the Provisional IRA, the IBA ordered them to scrap the whole programme. The team still went ahead, though dropping film of IRA training sessions and a mooted interview with IRA leader David O'Connell. The IBA again banned the newly completed film. IBA Chairperson Lady Plowden finally decided to allow it to be transmitted on 21 May, three weeks after its planned transmission date.

May 1978 - BBC
THE CITY ON THE BORDER AND THE IRISH WAY: 'A Bridge of Sorts'
The City on the Border, about Derry, was intended as a preface to the seven-part series, *The Irish Way*. Director Colin Thomas was already worried about the fact that the role of the British army went unquestioned in the film, when he learnt that two sections had been cut: one showed a tombstone which read 'Murdered by British Paratroopers on Bloody Sunday'. In the meantime, one

of the two films Thomas had directed in *The Irish Way* series 'A Bridge of Sorts', had been referred to BBC Northern Ireland, who said the film and commentary had to be substantially changed before transmission. Thomas refused to make the changes, and resigned. The film was transmitted under a new title, 'A Rock in the Road', with the changes.

June 1978 - Thames
THIS WEEK: 'The Amnesty Report'
Thames planned to transmit on 8 June a programme about the Amnesty report on the ill-treatment of suspects by the RUC. The report had already been widely leaked. The IBA banned the programme. The local ACTT union shop blacked the screening of a substitute programme, and the TV screen remained blank. Extracts from the shot film were subsequently shown on the BBC's *Nationwide*.

August 1978 - Southern
SPEARHEAD: 'Jackal'
Ulster TV refused to screen the fourth episode of this seven-part drama series about an army battalion. Like the first episode, which Ulster TV had screened, the fourth episode was set in the North of Ireland. The network transmission date, 8 August, coincided with the anniversary of the introduction of internment. This was the first time a drama programme, as opposed to current affairs, had been dropped by Ulster TV.

August 1978 - BBC
PLAY FOR TODAY: 'The Legion Hall Bombing'
This play, showing the operation of the Diplock Court system and based on the transcripts of the trial of Willie Gallagher, was scheduled for transmission on 23 February and was repeatedly postponed. The BBC insisted on commentary changes and that the epilogue completely dropped. The play was meant to be followed by a discussion, but this too was dropped. The play was transmitted on 22 August at the late time of 10.25 pm, instead of the usual *Play for Today* time of 9.25 pm. The director, Roland Joffé, and writer Caryl Churchill requested the removal of their names from the credits.

1979 - Granada
WORLD IN ACTION
An interview with republican spokesperson Danny Morris was dropped from a *World in Action* film on the North after Northern Ireland Secretary Howard Atkins said he would refuse to appear unless the interview was excluded.

May 1979 - Yorkshire TV
GLOBAL VILLAGE
IBA and Yorkshire TV officials forced the removal of an interview with Sinn Fein President Ruairi O Bradaigh from David Frost's *Global Village* programme on Northern Ireland. The cut was made because several Westminster MPs had walked out when they heard that O Bradaigh was due to appear. The programme normally went out live, but this one was recorded and previewed by the IBA because it dealt with the North of Ireland.

August 1979 - BBC
THE VANISHING ARMY
A repeat showing of this play, about an army sergeant who had become disillusioned after being wounded in the North of Ireland, was cancelled because of the Mountbatten and Warrenpoint killings. Playwright Robert Holles described the cancellation as 'a crude and crass piece of censorship'. The play was eventually repeated on 3 April 1980.

November 1979 - BBC
PANORAMA
As part of a film assessing the Provisional Republican movement on its tenth anniversary, *Panorama* filmed an IRA roadblock in Carrickmore, Co. Tyrone. This led to an outcry in Parliament and in the press. The film was seized by Scotland Yard acting under the Prevention of Terrorism Act. The BBC fired the *Panorama* editor Roger Bolton, reinstating him after union pressure. The programme was never completed.

November 1979 - BBC Northern Ireland
SPOTLIGHT
Spotlight, a BBC Northern Ireland local current affairs programme, planned to look at the implications of the *Panorama* 'Carrickmore' affair. The programme was banned at the last minute. *Spotlight* intended to bring together three journalists and three politicians to discuss the issue. Ironically, the official reason for the banning was the BBC's refusal to provide a spokesperson.

March 1980 - Harlech
CURIOUS JOURNEY
Harlech TV banned Kenneth Griffith's documentary, *Curious Journey*, which centred on interviews with Irish veterans of 1916 and 1918. Harlech wanted Griffith to cut several quotations from historical figures: one such was from the British Prime Minister William Gladstone, roundly condemning the 1800 Act of Union between Britain and Ireland. Griffith refused to make the cuts, and Harlech eventually sold him the film rights for £1.

50

March 1980 - BBC
GONE FOR A SOLDIER
On 9 March Philip Donnellan's film about the history of the British army seen through the eyes of ordinary soldiers, and including sequences in the North of Ireland, was shown on BBC2. An ensuing row in the House of Commons led to the BBC banning both repeats and foreign sales of the film.

June 1980 - Thames
CREGGAN
Transmission of this film about Derry, by Mary Holland and Michael Whyte, was delayed nearly a year. It was finally shown on 17 June with two cuts and a commentary alteration. Although it won the prestigious Prix Italia, and was named the best documentary of 1980 by the British Broadcasting Guild, it has not been repeated.

April 1981 - Thames
TV EYE: 'The Waiting Time'
This film, shown on 30 April, was about events immediately preceding the death of Bobby Sands MP. The IBA forced the producers to cut a 33-second sequence showing IRA members making a statement in a West Belfast social club and receiving rapturous applause.

June 1981 - Granada
WORLD IN ACTION: 'The Propaganda War'
Granada withdrew this film rather than comply with the IBA's command to excise a 27-second sequence showing hunger striker Patsy O'Hara lying in his coffin surrounded by an INLA guard of honour. The IBA apparently felt that the pictures might have invested those shown with a status they did not merit and would have given the 'wrong impression' to a British audience. Ironically, part of the offending sequence was transmitted several times in an advance promotion for the programme.

September 1981 - BBC
TOP OF THE POPS
The BBC banned a video made by the rock group Police to accompany their single *Invisible Sun* and due to be shown on *Top of the Pops* on 24 September. *The Times* described it as, 'A collage of Ulster street scenes incorporating urchins, graffiti, Saracens and soldiers ...it seemed good-hearted and utterly uncontentious' (16 December 1981). ATV showed a short clip of the video on *Tiswas*, omitting all references to Belfast.

January 1982 - BBC
OPEN DOOR
Senior BBC executives banned the Campaign for Free Speech on Ireland from making a programme for the BBC2 access slot, *Open Door*. The *Open Door* selection committee had approved the Campaign's application in November 1979. The project was 'referred up' to senior executives, including the Managing Director of BBC TV, the Controller of BBC2, and the Director of News and Current Affairs and Controller Northern Ireland. Three independent observers who sit on the *Open Door* selection committee wrote to the BBC to complain about the ban.

March 1983 - Yorkshire Television
FIRST TUESDAY
Yorkshire Television management ordered an end to work on a *First Tuesday* documentary on plastic bullets. Several months research had already been done and filming was due to start the following week. The ban came after the RUC and the IBA had put pressure on Yorkshire TV, following the appearance of an article about the programme in the Belfast paper, *The Irish News*.

October 1983 - Channel 4
THE CAUSE OF IRELAND
Shown in the *Eleventh Hour* slot on 3 October, *The Cause of Ireland* was largely funded by Channel 4. Made by Chris Reeves, a main theme was that Catholic and Protestant workers in the North cannot be united prior to reunification. Jeremy Isaacs, head of Channel 4, approved the completed film, but members of the IBA personally asked to see it and subsequently demanded that two pieces of commentary and two sequences be cut: a total of six minutes. The first commentary cut was: 'For, while the firepower of republicanism is usually aimed at the security forces or public representatives of the British state, loyalist violence has been directed indiscriminately at the Catholic community.' The second referred to the possibility of bloodshed after a British withdrawal: 'those Protestants who have been trained in the UDR and the RUC would remain a real threat to Catholics in the North of Ireland.' The two sequences are believed to have been removed after Northern Ireland CBA chief Richard Gordon and landowner Bill Montgomery put pressure on the IBA. The first, demonstrating the gap between rich and poor in the North, showed Montgomery and other gentry foxhunting in County Down. The second was an interview with Gordon, who stressed that normal activities like 'playing golf' continued despite the troubles.

Note: This list is partly based on the chronology by Paul Madden in ed. Campaign for Free Speech on Ireland, *The British Media and Ireland: Truth the First Casualty*, London: Information on Ireland 1979, pp 17-20.

1983 - Thames
TV EYE
According to a report in the Dublin *Sunday Tribune*, Thames TV's TV Eye compiled a programme in 1983 on cross-border activities by the British army and RUC, including alleged murders and attempted kidnappings. At the time, the *Tribune* reported, it was suspected that political pressure from prime minister Margaret Thatcher's office was responsible for blocking the programme. But this was now denied by Barry Sales, Thames TV's news and current affairs director: 'He said that the researchers had failed to come up with a story but refused to say if they had established evidence of cross-border activities by British security forces' (*Sunday Tribune*, 29 April 1984).

December 1983 - Channel 4
RIGHT TO REPLY
The week before Christmas, Channel 4's *Right to Reply* planned a studio confrontation between Gerry Adams MP and John Ware of Granada TV's *World in Action,* in which Adams would have made detailed criticisms of a film about himself made by Ware. Titled 'The Honourable Member for West Belfast', Ware's film was transmitted on ITV on 19 December 1983, two days after the IRA's bombing of Harrods. But as Philip Schlesinger explained in the *New Statesman,* 'In the aftermath of the bombing it was decided no such programme could be screened, thus forestalling a major political row in which the channel would undoubtedly have faced accusations of treason' (*New Statesman*, 6 January 1984).

December 1983 - Channel 4
SATURDAY NIGHT AT THE LONDON PALLADIUM
BEAT THE CLOCK and ENGLAND
Also in the aftermath of the Harrods bombing, Channel 4 banned several comedy sequences. Two cuts were made to old programmes featured in the *Comedy Classics* slot on 27 December 1983. A running gag featuring Norman Wisdom and Bruce Forsyth, during which Wisdom made repeated attempts to sing 'When Irish Eyes are Smiling', was cut from a rerun of *Saturday Night at the London Palladium* from 1961. Also cut was part of *Beat the Clock,* in which a passing reference was made to the North of Ireland.

Another comedy show to be cut was Paul Hogan's *England,* shown on 30 December. A sequence in which someone tried to steal a Harrods bag was removed, as was another in which a tourist asked the way to Harrods (*New Statesman*, 6 January 1984).

January 1984 - Yorkshire TV
JIMMY YOUNG SHOW
The producers of Yorkshire TV's Jimmy Young chat show arranged for Gerry Adams MP to appear as a guest on the programme to be transmitted on 15 January. According to the *Sunday Times*, 'although Adams's contribution was going to be carefully balanced with other political views, Young refused to do the interview on the grounds that Sinn Fein should not be allowed airtime on British TV' (*Sunday Times*, 15 January 1984). It is, however, possible that Jimmy Young initially agreed to have Adams on the show: Sinn Fein spokespersons said that the arrangements made by Yorkshire TV to accommodate Adams - which included altering the day on which the programme was to be recorded, and arranging special flights - were so complex that they were unlikely to have been made without Young's knowledge.

Following the Jimmy Young ban, Gerry Adams was invited for an interview on David Frost's breakfast programme on TV AM - an invitation which was angrily attacked by Tory MPs - and appeared on 15 January 1984.

January 1984 - Channel 4
GREEN FLUTES
Another victim of Channel 4's post-Harrods panic was *Green Flutes*, a documentary by Nancy Schiesari about a republican flute band from Glasgow, which was scheduled for transmission in the *Eleventh Hour* slot on 16 January 1984. Channel 4 executives decided - apparently when the commissioning editor was away - to take the film out of the schedules, and it way finally transmitted on 5 March. The film had previously been delayed twice. A transmission date was first promised for September 1983, but then cuts were demanded - and made - in sequences shot in the North of Ireland. It was then due to be shown in December 1983, but was replaced by a programme about the Clyde, which was then topical.

September 1984 - London Weekend
WEEKEND WORLD: 'From the Shadow of a Gun'
On Sunday 16 September 1984, London Weekend's *Weekend World* slot carried the fourth and final part of a documentary titled 'From the Shadow of a Gun', presented by Mary Holland. The planned format was that former diplomat Nicholas Henderson would take the role of honest broker and interview members of the various political parties in the North of Ireland. But Henderson refused to sit down with Sinn Fein, so LWT offered Sinn Fein a separate interview, done by Mary Holland. Sinn Fein decided not to appear on this basis, and issued a statement on 14 September 1984 saying, 'Sinn Fein sees no reason why it should participate in this programme in a way

which depicts republicans as political lepers, and considers that *Weekend World* has surrendered objectivity and independence to the political narrowmindedness of Nicholas Henderson.'

February 1985 - Channel 4/RTE
THE PRICE
The Price was a six-part thriller, shown on Channel 4 and RTE in January and February 1985, about a woman being kidnapped by a republican 'terrorist' organisation. Top Belfast actor Mark Holland played the part of an RUC Special Branch detective. In the last episode, according to the script, the detective took part in a shoot-out south of the border. But then, according to Holland, his part was dropped from the last episode on RUC instructions, because they did not want even a fictional character acting the part of an RUC officer to be seen operating south of the border. 'I was contracted to do the final episode,' said Holland, 'but I was told by the executive producer that the RUC didn't want me in it' (*Sunday Press*, 17 February 1985).

May 1985 - BBC
PANORAMA
A *Panorama* programme critical of policing in the North of Ireland was delayed for a year. The *Irish News* of 12 August 1985 reported that the BBC had 'torpedoed' the programme some three months earlier, on advice from its lawyers. The paper said that the programme 'dealt with Catholic claims that the RUC operated a shoot to kill policy.' The journalists were looking at 'the controversial double killing of Armagh INLA members Seamus Grew and Roddy Carroll in December 1982', and 'were also probing the Stalker Report on the RUC which had been leaked to them.' The programme was finally shown on 16 June 1986.

July 1985 - BBC
REAL LIVES: 'At the Edge of the Union'
One of the biggest rows of the 1980s was over this *Real Lives* programme about the political and personal lives of two Derry politicians, republican Martin McGuinness and loyalist Gregory Campbell. The programme, produced by Paul Hamann, was scheduled for 7 August 1985. On 28 July the *Sunday Times* carried a report titled 'Thatcher slams IRA film', and alleged that McGuinness was chief of staff of the IRA. The BBC had vetted the film through its internal censorship procedures, and executives defended the decision to show it. Then on Monday 29 July the home secretary, Leon Brittan, wrote to the BBC saying the film - which he hadn't seen - was 'contrary to the national interest' and likely to give 'succour to terrorist organisations'.

On Tuesday 30 July the BBC's governors held a special day-long meeting, viewed the programme, and decided to ban it, thus violating the usual relationship between them and the board of management.

This capitulation to political pressure and flagrant abandonment of the BBC's much-vaunted independence from government caused a major public outcry. The level of shock is difficult to appreciate today, several years after the introduction of the broadcasting ban, since the public is now acclimatised to the notion of overt government dictatorship over the broadcasters.

The National Union of Journalists called a 24-hour protest stoppage on 7 July, and won almost total support from broadcasters. No national news was broadcast in Britain on 7 August, and the BBC World Service broadcast music all day. The *Times* reported:

> 'The walkout by journalists and technical staff represented the most serious industrial action ever undertaken in British television, and attracted more support than has ever been won by a pay claim or a call for conventional industrial action.

> 'The BBC was reduced to basic services without news on all television and radio, national and local, and independent television was without its national news service, ITN, and most regional news and current affairs programmes on all but five stations' (Times, 8 August 1985).

On the day of the strike, BBC director general Alasdair Milne said that the film would be shown in due course, but needed some amendment. On 5 September a joint statement from the governors and the board of management announced that the film would be shown in October with three small amendments. The main amendment was the addition of a 20-second colour film sequence of the aftermath of the IRA's 'Bloody Friday' bombings in Belfast in 1972, showing bodies being carried away. Two amendments concerned changes to captions. No cuts were made. The film was eventually transmitted on 16 October 1985.

July 1985 - BBC
OPEN SPACE: 'On the Word of a Supergrass'
An article in the *Guardian* on 31 July, in the middle of the *Real Lives* controversy, revealed that Brian Wenham, the BBC's director of programmes, had told the independent producers of 'On the Word of a Supergrass' that the programme would be postponed from its scheduled date of 14 August, possibly to 18 September. The *Guardian* reported: 'It is understood that Mr Wenham was concerned that, whether or not the interview with the alleged IRA chief of staff, Martin McGuinness, was allowed to be shown, a programme on the

56

sensitive subject of supergrasses should not go out only a week later.'

On the Word of a Supergrass' was eventually transmitted on 19 September.

July 1985 - BBC Scotland
OPEN TO QUESTION
In the midst of the *Real Lives* row, on 31 July 1985, Sinn Fein publicised the fact that Gerry Adams had been sent an invitation by a researcher at BBC Scotland to appear on *Open to Question*, a discussion slot in which public figures were questioned by teenagers. Sinn Fein announced that Gerry Adams was accepting the invitation. A BBC spokesman told the press that the programme's producers had failed to follow the procedure of referring upwards any programme in which a member of Sinn Fein was to appear, to obtain the approval of senior management (*Daily Telegraph, Star*, 1 August 1985). *Open to Question* never subsequently made a programme featuring Gerry Adams.

August 1985 - BBC Radio Manchester
IRISH LINE
Four members of the production team of *Irish Line*, a weekly programme made (without pay) by the Irish in Britain Representation Group for BBC Radio Manchester, accused the BBC in August 1985 of censoring the programme. In a letter to the *Irish Post*, the paper of the Irish community in Britain, they listed items that had been censored. These included the cutting of two questions from an interview with an Irishwoman who was chairperson of the SDP in Manchester: one asked why she had joined the IBRG, while the other asked what was SDP policy on the presence of British troops in the North of Ireland. The BBC also cut out of a What's On' section an announcement of a Labour Party Young Socialists public meeting on strip-searching in Armagh jail. The BBC also cut completely a prerecorded interview about strip-searching with Bernadette Hyland, and IBRG member of the International Women's Day delegation to Armagh, which made an annual protest outside the then women's prison. This item was cut on 24 April, and the programme started six minutes late as a result (*Irish Post*, 10 August 1985).

November 1985 - UTV
WITNESS
On 29 November 1985, UTV refused to screen a five-minute religious broadcast by David Bleakley, general secretary of the Irish Council of Churches. In the broadcast, he warned of the dangers of endemic fear in Northern Ireland and said that what was needed was 'a politics of doing things together'. UTV said that the programme was in contravention of a section of

the Broadcasting Act' and said it hoped to screen the edition in a later subsequent current affairs programme. David Bleakley said he was 'dumbfounded' at the decision. He was trying to provide a 'vision of reassurance and reconciliation' (*Irish Times*, 30 November 1985).

December 1985 - ITV
CHRISTMAS EVE MASS

Christmas Eve Mass, celebrated by Bishop Cathal Daly, was due to be broadcast from the Mater Hospital, Belfast. Shortly before transmission time, it was announced that the programme had been changed and another programme, recorded a year or two previously, was screened instead. No reason was given for the change.

December 1985 - BBC
SONGS OF PRAISE

Angry Protestants forced the BBC to scrap plans for a cross-community edition of *Songs of Praise* from Dungannon, County Tyrone. The BBC's plan was for Dungannon Protestants and Catholics to join together in a service in the Catholic Church of St Patrick. The BBC had planned to record the programme on the two days immediately prior to the 23 January 1986 by-elections, sparked by the resignation of the Northern Unionist Westminster MPs, who were protesting against the recently signed Anglo-Irish Agreement. Anger at the Anglo-Irish Agreement was thought to be the cause of the Protestants' unwillingness to co-operate with *Songs of Praise*. Father Skelly, head of religious programmes for BBC Northern Ireland, said that Dungannon was the first area where he had found any opposition to the programme, which had been recorded in Larne, Limavady, Strabane and Letterkenny with good support from both sections in the community' (*Irish News*, 31 December 1985).

January 1986 - BBC
QUESTION TIME

The BBC scrapped plans for a *Question Time* to be broadcast from Belfast on 30 January 1986, shortly after the by-elections provoked by Unionist MPs resigning in protest at the recently signed Anglo-Irish agreement. Those invited to take part included Tom King, the secretary of state for Northern Ireland, and Peter Barry, minister for foreign affairs for the Republic of Ireland. The *Irish News* reported: 'It is thought that unionist politicians, currently refusing to speak to Mr King, would have been reluctant to take part in the broadcast, leaving the programme-makers with problems over balancing content' (*Irish News*, 18 January 1986). SDLP MP Eddie McGrady accused the BBC of bowing to pressure from loyalist bigots.

December 1986 - Channel 4
ELEVENTH HOUR: 'Turn it Up/They Shoot to Kill Children'
On 8 December 1986 the IBA, with the agreement of Channel 4's management, banned a 14-minute video about the use of plastic bullets in the North of Ireland. The video, titled 'They Shoot to Kill Children', was due to be shown late that night in the *Eleventh Hour* slot at the end of a compilation of videos made by groups of young people. The compilation, titled 'Turn It Up', was put together by the Birmingham Film and Video Workshop. The banned video included an interview with Paul Corr, who was hit in the face by a plastic bullet in 1981 when he was 12 years old, and a song which mentioned 14 of those killed by rubber and plastic bullets.

March 1987 - BBC
CROSSFIRE
This five-part thriller serial was referred back to the BBC in London for changes by James Hawthorne, the BBC's Northern Ireland controller. He was believed to have asked for the series' final two parts to be reshot. He said he had not previously been consulted by the programme's makers and, having viewed it, found it gave too sympathetic a portrayal of the IRA and an unfavourable depiction of the security forces. The programme had taken over two years to make, at a cost of over £1 million. Due to be screened from 6 March 1987, it finally went out from 15 March 1988.

In April 1988 actor Tony Doyle, who played the IRA chief of staff in the series, revealed that he had to redub certain lines in the script on the insistence of the RUC. He said: 'In one line I said "The organisation has safe houses in Belfast." I had to change that to "The organisation has bridgeheads in Belfast." They are of the opinion that there are no safe houses in Belfast' (*Sunday Press*, 10 April 1988).

December 1987 - Channel 4
COURT REPORT: 'The Birmingham Six'
On 3 December 1987, the attorney-general was granted an injunction by the Court of Appeal preventing Channel 4 from broadcasting that night a dramatised version of the appeal hearing of the Birmingham Six. The Court of Appeal, which consisted of the lord chief justice, Lord Lane, and two other judges, was the same court that was currently hearing the Birmingham Six's appeal, depicted in the dramatisation. On 16 December, the three judges refused to lift the injunction. They finally lifted in on 29 January 1988, after they had rejected the Birmingham Six's appeal, and Channel 4 cleared the schedules to show the two-hour programme that evening.

January 1988 - Channel 4
ACCEPTABLE LEVELS
Channel 4 chief Michael Grade pulled *Acceptable Levels* from the schedules on 28 January 1988 because he felt it would be 'inappropriate' to screen it on the day of the verdict in the Birmingham Six appeal. Ironically the film examines media self-censorship: it tells the story of how a TV team reacts when a child they are filming in Divis Flats is killed by a British soldier's plastic bullet. *Acceptable Levels* had been shown before on Channel 4 , on 30 April 1984. Its suppression was discussed in a *Right to Reply* programme in February 1988. It was finally transmitted on 18 February 1988.

April 1988 - London Weekend
ABC OF BRITISH MUSIC
A scene showing the killing of a British soldier was removed from the *ABC of British Music*, directed by Ken Russell, after the killing of two soldiers who drove into a republican funeral parade in Belfast. The scene accompanied the Pogues singing 'The Ballad of the Gentleman Soldier'. It depicted a soldier bringing a girl into a sentry box. Soon after the girl leaves, the sentry box explodes. Instead the scene, to be shown on Easter Saturday, just showed the sentry box 'wobbling about a bit'. The Pogues were included under I for Ireland.

April 1988 - Channel 4
FRIDAY NIGHT LIVE: The Pogues
The Pogues accused Channel 4 of censoring one of their songs and said they would not appear on the channel again. They were performing their song 'Streets of Sorrow/Birmingham Six' live when they were cut off two-thirds of the way through by a commercial break. The programme's producer denied that it was censorship and said the artists had to be kept to a very exact time. The Pogues' manager complained that no-one cuts off comedians before the punch-line, nor are boxing or football matches cut off before the end just because a commercial break was on the way. He said he believed the programme had several minutes to spare before the end, which the presenters had to fill by ad libbing (*Irish Post*, 7 May 1988).

** A major storm blew up in April and May 1988 over Thames TV's *This Week* programme 'Death on the Rock', which cast doubts on the government's version of what happened when the SAS killed three IRA members in Gibraltar in March 1988. On 28 April foreign secretary Geoffrey Howe asked Lord Thompson, chair of the IBA, to postpone the programme until after the inquest in Gibraltar. The IBA refused, and the programme was broadcast on 5 May. Following transmission, prime minister Thatcher, Northern Ireland secretary

Tom King, and much of the press, accused Thames TV of 'trial by television'. Thames TV subsequently initiated an independent inquiry into the programme under Lord Windlesham: the inquiry concluded that it was appropriate that the programme was made.

June 1988 - Channel 4
NETWORK 7
When *Network 7*, a trendy Channel 4 magazine programme which was normally transmitted live, planned to broadcast a live discussion on 'Should the troops remain in Ireland?', the IBA demanded that the programme should be prerecorded a few hours earlier to allow them to vet the tapes before transmission. The programme had commissioned a poll on 'troops out' that revealed 57 per cent in favour and 43 per cent against. A planned live phone-in poll was dropped after pressure from the IBA, who claimed it would be 'open to abuse by unrepresentative opinion'. Such polls were standard practice on *Network 7*.

August 1988 - BBC
ELEPHANT, MONKEYS and NIGHTWATCH
In the wake of the Ballygawley bus bombing, in which eight British soldiers were killed, the BBC announced on 23 August 1988 that it was postponing three plays made by BBC Northern Ireland, saying it was 'inappropriate to show such plays at this time'. *Elephant* was a play without dialogue, re-enacting a series of killings in the North of Ireland. *Nightwatch* was about freelance intelligence services in Amsterdam and mercenaries in Africa. *Monkeys* reproduced parts of the court hearings of failed car manufacturer John de Lorean, when he faced charges of drug dealing. The three plays were finally shown over three weeks starting on 25 January 1989.

September 1988 - Channel 4
AFTER DARK WITH GERRY ADAMS MP
On 8 October 1988 Professor Paul Wilkinson of Aberdeen University publicised and protested against the fact that Gerry Adams MP was to appear in *After Dark*'s live late-night discussion show on 10 October. The programme-makers had asked Wilkinson for advice on contacts, but had not asked him to appear. Wilkinson's protest led to angry attacks on Channel 4 by Tory MPs. Liz Forgan, Channel 4's director of programmes, decided that the programme should be abandoned, claiming that a 'satisfactory context' for Adams' appearance could not be found at such short notice. Forgan thus avoided a confrontation with the IBA, which said that if necessary it would have used Section 4 of the Broadcasting Act to stop Adams appearing (*Guardian*, 19 September 1988).

October 1988 - BBC
PANORAMA ON THE SAS

A *Panorama* programme on the role of the SAS in the North of Ireland, due to be shown on 3 October 1988, was postponed after the BBC's director general Michael Checkland and his deputy John Birt had viewed it. A BBC spokesman said that they had taken the decision on the grounds that the programme 'needed a bit more doing on it' (*Guardian*, 3 October 1988). The programme was shown on 17 October after cuts and changes had been made. Parts of an SAS training video showing an exercise in the regiment's 'killing house' was removed on the advice of Admiral William Higgins, secretary to the D-notice committee. The scene showed SAS soldiers in balaclavas using live bullets to rescue a hostage held by the IRA.

October 1988 -
The Broadcasting Ban

The broadcasting ban on eleven Irish organisations was formally announced by the home secretary, Douglas Hurd, on 19 October 1988. He issued 'notices' to the BBC and IBA under, respectively, clause 14(4) of the BBC's licence and agreement, and section 29(3) of the Broadcasting Act 1981. This legislation was designed for use in wartime, and empowers the home secretary to ban the broadcasting of any matter he specifies. This power has since been included in the 1990 Broadcasting Act, which covers cable and satellite services as well as the commercial television channels.

The ban prevents to broadcasting of words spoken by representatives of eleven organisations, and of words spoken in support of those organisations. When the ban was introduced, three of the affected organisations were legal - Sinn Fein, Republican Sinn Fein, and the Ulster Defence Association - but the UDA was subsequently outlawed. The ban also covers all organisations banned under the Emergency Provisions Act or the Prevention of Terrorism Act. These are now: the IRA, the INLA, Cumann na mBan, Fianna Eireann, the Red Hand Commandos, Saor Eire (long since defunct), the Ulster Freedom Fighters, the Ulster Volunteer Force, and the UDA.

The ban does not affect proceedings in parliament, where freedom of speech is guaranteed by parliamentary privilege, which was established by the Bill of Rights of 1689. Also, its effects are eased during election periods, when coverage of candidates is safeguarded by the Representation of the People Act. Consequently, during election periods broadcasters can transmit the voices of candidates and their supporters, regardless of their party.

The Response to the Ban

Broadcasters responded very nervously to the ban, moving immediately to alter plans that had been made for interviews and programmes. They interpreted the ban very broadly, applying it to people who were not members of the listed groups, nor advocating support for those groups. Any opposition to government policy on Irish affairs became suspect. The ban rapidly became a routine element in broadcasters' thinking, conditioning their decisions on whom to invite for interview and what programmes to make.

Radio

Radio - not covered in this chronology - was immediately and heavily affected by the ban, in part because organisations which challenge British policy on Ireland

- like other pressure groups - had up till then had easier access to radio than to television.

In the immediate aftermath of the ban, local radio stations both in the North of Ireland and in Britain applied it indiscriminately. Those who found themselves silenced included not only representatives of Sinn Fein, but also Errol Smalley, uncle of Paul Hill of the Guildford Four; Bernadette Devlin McAliskey; Richard Stanton, a Brighton Labour councillor and member of the Troops Out Movement; and US author Margie Bernard, author of *Daughter of Derry*, and the subject of her book, Brigid Sheils Makowski.

Also silenced were three pop groups. The Pogues' song 'Streets of Sorrow/ Birmingham Six' - which proclaimed the innocence of the Birmingham Six and the Guildford Four - was banned by the Independent Broadcasting Authority (see below, November 1988). Dingle Spike's rendering of 'The Bold Fenian Men' was reportedly banned by Radio Tay in Dundee. Also, That Petrol Emotion were told that the song 'Cellophane' from their recent album could not be played on radio or TV.

Television News

Television news coverage within the North of Ireland and nationally has been severely affected by the ban. This chronology does not cover news bulletins, but a survey of the effects of the ban on British national television news has been done by the Glasgow University Media Group. Titled *Speak No Evil*, the study compared the coverage in the year following the ban (18 October 1988 to 19 October 1989) to the previous year's coverage.

The survey found that following the ban the number of Sinn Fein appearances on national British news dropped by more than 63 per cent, to 34. Of these, 20 were in items about violence - and nine were about the ban itself!

The effects of the ban on broadcasting within the North of Ireland have undoubtedly been very severe. Prior to the ban Sinn Fein appeared frequently, but is now rarely approached.

Guidelines

Broadcasting chiefs issued a succession of guidelines on how staff should interpret the ban. On 24 October 1988, in response to a query from the BBC, C L Scoble from the broadcasting department of the Home Office issued a detailed clarification. This stated that voiceover accounts of the words of affected people were permissible, as were reconstructions of actual events using actors. It also stated that the ban would not apply to members of listed organisation when they were speaking in a personal capacity or purely in their capacity as a member of an organisation not covered by the ban, such as an elected council. (See *BBC Producer's Guidelines*, available from BBC shops.)

Voiceovers and Subtitles

Since the ban, the actual voices of Sinn Fein representatives have only been broadcast on television or radio in special circumstances. These have included situations where the person was not speaking as a Sinn Fein representative - for instance, Gerry Adams speaking in his (former) capacity as MP for West Belfast; and during election campaigns, when the rights of candidates and their supporters are legally protected.

The actual voices of Sinn Fein members (as opposed to representatives) have been heard more often. Prominent members whose voices have been broadcast on national television include Rita O'Hare interviewed in Channel 4's *Mother Ireland* (see below, April 1991) and Joe Cahill, who had the curious distinction of speaking with two different voices on the BBC's *Timewatch* (see below, January 1993).

Most interviews with Sinn Fein representatives are now broadcast with the person's original voice removed, and replaced either with a reporter's voiceover, or with subtitles, or with an actor's voice. In some cases, programme-makers have gone to great lengths to ensure that the actor's voice is accurately dubbed and similar to the original.

Subtitles have also been used over people who are neither members nor representatives of Sinn Fein, including the Pogues (subtitled singing their banned song 'Streets of Sorrow/Birmingham Six' on ITN), and Bernadette McAliskey on the BBC's *Nation* discussion programme (see below, September 1992).

There have been hardly any censored interviews with representatives of loyalist paramilitary organisations. Only one instance - a *Spotlight* interview with UDA leader Tommy Lyttle in October 1989 - is featured in this chronology. The Glasgow University Media Group did not find a single example in their survey of national news in the year after the ban.

Legal Challenges

At the time of writing, autumn 1993, there are three legal challenges to the broadcasting ban in progress.

The first, backed by the National Union of Journalists, BECTU and the anti-censorship campaign Article 19, is being taken to the European Court of Human Rights in Strasbourg, having been rejected by the British courts. This case is being brought by six journalists and a member of the NUJ's staff. They are claiming that the ban is unlawful, perverse and in breach of the European

Convention on Human Rights. Their case has been rejected by the High Court, the Court of Appeal and the House of Lords.

The second challenge is being made by Derry Sinn Fein councillor Mitchel McLaughlin, and is also going to the European Court of Human Rights. Cllr McLaughlin is claiming that the ban violates his right under Article 10 of the European Convention to receive and impart information without interference by a public authority. In September 1989, he lost a judicial review of the ban. He then went to the Court of Appeal in Belfast. His case came up in March 1991, soon after the House of Lords had rejected the similar action backed by the NUJ. Cllr McLaughlin's barrister, Seamus Treacy, therefore said there would be no point in appealing, and asked the court to dismiss the appeal, which it did. This move exhausted the domestic remedies, allowing the case to go to Europe.

The third challenge is being made by Bernadette Devlin McAliskey, following the BBC's decision to subtitle her contribution to the discussion programme *Nation* (see below, September 1992, for details).

After the Ban

October 1988 - Channel 4
MOTHER IRELAND

Mother Ireland, a 52-minute video made by Derry Film & Video and funded by Channel 4, was the first television programme to fall victim to the ban. The video explores the personification of Ireland as a woman in Irish culture and nationalism. Among the many women interviewed are historian Margaret MacCurtain, journalist Nell McCafferty, film-maker Pat Murphy, Cumann na mBan veterans Sighle Humphries and Miriam James, and Mairead Farrell (shot dead by the SAS in Gibraltar in March 1988). There is also old film of the legendary activist Maud Gonne addressing a rally.

For several months before the ban, Channel 4 had been requesting alterations to the video. They wanted the removal of film by Emma Groves immediately after she was shot in the fact by a rubber bullet fired by a British soldier in 1971, and also of Christy Moore's song 'Unfinished Revolution', and of a montage of Irish women in resistance roles. Just before the ban, Channel 4 demanded more changes, including the removal of the interview with Mairead Farrell.

On 2 November Channel 4 issued a statement saying that the ban 'made further discussion on such a version academic, for it was clear that under any legal interpretation, the ban would rule out many other sections of the programme, including contributions from elderly participants in the 1920s Civil War'. This view was in line with advice issued by Don Christopher of Channel 4's legal services on 24 October: 'The ban is not limited to material produced or recorded after 19 October. It would cover any such material recorded at any time in the past - for example newsreel footage shot before the creation of the Republic of Ireland.'

In February 1989, *Mother Ireland* won the 'best documentary' award at a major international women's film festival, Femmes Cathodiques, in Paris. It was shown widely in Europe, the USA, Australia and New Zealand, and was bought by the West German station WDR and by Basque television.

The footage of Emma Groves after she was shot by a rubber bullet was shown on BBC2 in May 1989 in the *Split Screen* slot, in a film made by Ken Loach for the Time to Go campaign.

Parts of Derry Film & Video's interview with Mairead Farrell - sections which had not been used in *Mother Ireland* - were shown on US television in June 1989, in the film *Death of a Terrorist* (see below).

Mother Ireland was eventually transmitted - although with alterations - by Channel 4 in April 1991 as part of its banned season (see below).

October 1988 - Channel 4

THE MEDIA SHOW

On 30 October 1988, Channel 4's *Media Show* carried an examination of the effects of the broadcasting ban. This included an interview with Derry Sinn Fein councillor Dodie McGuinness, whose voice was silenced and replaced with another voice repeating exactly what she had said. Cllr McGuinness had explained how the ban made it impossible for her to use the media to get publicity for the council's campaign against the closure of a local maternity unit.

Introducing her censored interview, a voiceover explained: 'Following legal advice, the senior management at Channel 4 thought this interview would be borderline but acceptable under the new notice. However, following its own legal advice, the Independent Broadcasting Authority thought it unacceptable. Since the IBA have the final say in what we broadcast, Channel 4 must abide by their ruling. Accordingly, all we can now do is tell you what Councillor McGuinness said'.

The local BBC radio station, Radio Foyle, took a different line, broadcasting an interview with Cllr McGuinness on 16 November 1988 with sound intact.

November 1988 - Commercial TV and radio

THE POGUES': 'Streets of Sorrow/Birmingham Six'

On 20 November 1988 the *Observer* revealed that the Independent Broadcasting Authority had issued a circular to all commercial radio stations saying that the Pogues' song 'Streets of Sorrow/Birmingham Six' should not be played. The song supported the pleas of innocence by the Birmingham Six and Guildford Four, who were then still imprisoned. The IBA said in a statement that, 'The song alleges some convicted terrorists are not guilty and goes on to suggest that Irish people are at a disadvantage in British courts of law. That allegation might support or solicit or invite support for an organisation proscribed by the Home Secretary's directive, in that they indicate a general disagreement with the way in which the British government responds to, and the courts deal with, the terrorist threat in the UK'.

The IBA's ban was made by its radio division and followed a request for a ruling on five songs by executives at Manchester's Piccadilly Radio. The IBA cleared the other four songs, one of which, ironically, was Paul McCartney's 'Give Ireland Back to the Irish', which was banned by the BBC in 1972. The IBA's director of television followed the ruling made by the radio division.

On 20 December 1988, in a news item on the NUJ's court case against the ban, ITN's 5.45 news bulletin referred to the Pogues ban. The Pogues were shown on stage, then over a freeze-frame a caption, accompanied by a voiceover, gave a version of the banned song:

> *There were six men in Birmingham*
> *In Guildford there's four*
> *That were picked up and tortured*
> *And framed by the law*
> *An the filth got promotion*
> *But they're still doing time*
> *For being Irish in the wrong place*
> *And at the wrong time.*

The IBA was subsequently replaced by two separate bodies, the Radio Authority and the Independent Television Commission. In 1991, after the freeing of the Birmingham Six, the Radio Authority lifted the ban on the song. The ITC does not have the same powers as the IBA had. It is not the legal broadcaster of the programme it regulates. It is now up to the licensee - the company with the franchise to broadcast to a particular area - to decide whether the song can be included in a programme. An ITC spokesperson explained: 'The ITC now only intervenes after the event if it feels there has been a breach. I think it is fair to say that it would be highly unlikely that the ITC would seek to intervene if the song were broadcast today' (letter to David Miller, Glasgow University Media Group, 17 March 1993).

December 1988 - BBC
40 MINUTES: 'Greenfinches'
After consultation with the Ministry of Defence, the BBC cut part of 'Greenfinches', a documentary about three women members of the Ulster Defence Regiment, transmitted on 1 December 1988. A BBC spokesman told the press that the programme could not have been made without the co-operation of the MoD: 'As a courtesy they were shown the film and voiced concern about the security aspects of one aspect of the programme. After due consideration we agreed to trim the voiceover' (*Irish News*, 25 November 1988). One section cut was reportedly a suggestion made by one of the UDR women 'that some UDR members join purely to get firearms training to fight a civil war against the Catholics, should the army be withdrawn' (*Independent*, 24 November 1988).

69

1989 - Channel 4
THE SILENT SCREAM (Originally Sixteen Dead)
The Silent Scream was a documentary about the use of plastic bullets in the North of Ireland commissioned by Channel 4 from Belfast Independent Video (now Northern Visions). It was made in close collaboration with relatives of those killed or injured by plastic bullets. All stages of production were monitored by Channel 4, to a second 'rough cut' edit, and pronounced satisfactory. But Channel 4 decided not to transmit the programme, giving as an official reason its 'lack of structure'. Unofficially, the programme-makers were told, 'We have to keep our heads low,' and 'Ireland is a sensitive issue'.

1989 - All channels
DEATH OF A TERRORIST
Death of a Terrorist is a documentary about the life of Mairead Farrell, one of three IRA members killed by the SAS in Gibraltar in March 1988. It was made by William Cran - a former BBC producer - for the Boston station WGBH's *Frontline* slot. WGBH is part of the Public Broadcasting Service network, which includes more than 200 US television stations. *Death of a*

Terrorist was shown on the PBS network on 13 June 1989. It was subsequently shown on NHK - Japan's equivalent of the BBC - and in some European countries. Executives from the BBC, Channel 4 and Thames TV asked to see *Death of a Terrorist*. All said they liked the programme and that it was a pity that it was unbroadcastable in Britain under the present rules. (See article by Roger Bolton in the *Listener*, 3 August 1989.)

The *New York Post* wrote on 14 June 1989: 'The first half of *Death of a Terrorist* is far from sentimental in its treatment of Mairead Farrell ... It also establishes, though, that the British Special Air Services took a "007" approach to those terrorists, and shot to kill - even though the IRA agents had been tracked for days, and were unarmed at the time of their ambush'.

March 1989 - BBC
HERE IS THE NEWS
The BBC ordered cuts in *Here is the News*, a thriller by G F Newman, which was transmitted on Sunday 5 March 1989. One section cut was a fragment of conversation between the attorney-general and a journalist which suggested that the prime minister knew the truth about the SAS killing of three members of the IRA in Gibraltar (*Guardian*, 3 March 1989).

May 1989 - Channel 4
ELEVENTH HOUR: 'Trouble the Calm'
Trouble the Calm', a film by Faction Films about political attitudes in the South of Ireland, was shown in Channel 4's *Eleventh Hour* slot on 8 May 1989. Channel 4 insisted that the film-makers cut about two minutes of an interview with a woman whose husband was imprisoned in Portlaoise, in which she explained why he had been jailed. The film-makers persuaded Channel 4 to allow them to replace the excised section with a caption, which read: 'Under government broadcasting restrictions, in force since October 1988, this woman cannot explain her husband's beliefs and motivations which led to his imprisonment in Portlaoise goal'.

June 1989 - Channel 4
DISPATCHES: 'A State of Decay'
This *Dispatches* programme, an assessment marking the twentieth anniversary of British troops being deployed in the North of Ireland, included a voiced-over interview with Gerry Adams MP. It was shown on 28 June 1989.

August-September 1989 - Thames

THE TROUBLES

From 17 August 1989, Thames TV repeated its acclaimed series on the history of the North of Ireland, *The Troubles*, in five weekly parts. The series had first been shown in January and February 1981. Due to the broadcasting ban, six pieces of sound that had been transmitted in 1981 were excised from the repeat and replaced with subtitles.

The censored items included interviews with Gerry Adams and Joe Cahill, both of Sinn Fein. In the fourth programme, prisoners' voices were censored in film shot in 1979 during the 'no wash' and 'blanket' protests, as was the voice of hunger'striker Raymond McCartney in an interview done by Granada TV's *World in Action* in November 1980. Subtitles replaced the voices of blanket men calling out, 'We're political prisoners. We want political status,' and 'Victory to the blanket men'. McCartney's captioned words were: 'The whole system in Northern Ireland, both special arrest, special court system without jury, has proved to us beyond all doubt that these courts are set up to convict men, just to convince people that we are criminals, which we are not. We are a product of the political troubles in Northern Ireland at this moment'.

August 1989 - BBC

FOREVER DIVIDED

Forever Divided, shown on 13 August 1989, was a 90-minute programme by Jonathon Dimbleby marking the twentieth anniversary of the deployment of troops. It included a subtitled interview with Gerry Adams MP. Talking about the IRA's 1984 bombing of Brighton's Grand Hotel, which prime minister Margaret Thatcher had described as a blow against democracy, Gerry Adams said (in subtitles): 'It was a blow for Irish democracy. It was an attempt to bring about the end of the British Cabinet, which was maintaining, undemocratically, the partition of this country, and which is now in charge of 20 unbroken years of direct military occupation' (*Independent*, 14 August 1989).

August 1989 - Channel 4

CREGGAN

On 22 August 1989, Channel 4 repeated the Thames TV film *Creggan* by Michael Whyte and Mary Holland, in a series of prize-winning Thames films. *Creggan*, about people on a Derry housing estate, had first been shown on 17 June 1980 after being delayed for ten months (see above). It won the Prix Italia but was not repeated at the time.

The repeat fell victim to the broadcasting ban. Four sections of sound were cut, from interviews with two women, and replaced by subtitles. These were:

First woman
Caption 1: '… and then somebody starts in the first place about having to become involved.'

Caption 2: 'I don't know, maybe I had a funny outlook on the Provisional IRA - but to me the Provisional IRA was a crowd of young fellows that just tried to pay back some of the brutality that they had got. This is the way I thought of it anyway. Now I don't agree with everything that the Provos done, I think very few people do. But at the same time I could understand how they felt, especially the young, very young fellows that were caught up in it.'

Second woman
Caption 1: 'He said that talking had never solved Derry's problem, that the politicians had done absolutely nothing and that the only way to get the British to leave the country was by the gun, that was the only language that they understood.'

Caption 2 (responding to the question, 'Do you regard the soldiers themselves as your enemy?'): 'Not the soldiers, but the uniform that they wear, there is a human being inside that uniform, I'm sure if I ever got talking to them that they could be quite friendly, but when he dons a uniform, to me he's my enemy.'

August 1989 - Visnews
On 23 August 1989, *Public Eye*, a current affairs programme on Australia's Channel 10, transmitted a critical film about the British broadcasting ban. It included a sequence showing how Maxine Mawhinney of the Belfast office of Visnews, the world's largest television news agency, now routinely made two versions of stories involving Sinn Fein. One version, without Sinn Fein voices, was for sale to Sky News for transmission to the UK. The other, with Sinn Fein voices, was for sale to television stations internationally. *Public Eye* used as an example Mawhinney's two versions of a report of Gerry Adams' address to Sinn Fein's annual conference.

September 1989 - BBC
BENTHAM/1996
The BBC insisted that G F Newman rewrite a play loosely based on the Stalker investigation of the RUC's 'shoot-to-kill' policy and the Kincora boys' home scandal. He had to change the setting from Ireland in the past to Wales in the future. The original version, a three-part series, was based on his book *The Testing Ground* and was titled *Bentham* after the central character. The new version, shown on 17 September 1989, was a single play titled *1996*.

73

September 1989 - Channel 4
DISPATCHES: 'A State of Decay' (repeat)
On 21 September 1989, Channel 4 repeated this *Dispatches* programme, first shown on 28 June, which included a voiced-over interview with Gerry Adams MP.

September 1989 - ITV
SARACEN
Following the IRA's bombing of a Marines barracks in Deal, Kent, on 22 September 1989, which killed 10 bandsmen, ITV postponed the episode of the thriller series *Saracen* due to be shown next night. The episode recounted events after one of the heroes, a former SAS man, took up with an Irish woman not realising he had killed one of her relations while serving in the North of Ireland. It was replaced by a story about a London bank robbery, and was transmitted later on 7 October.

September 1989 - BBC
THE SQUAD
This programme, about the West Midlands Serious Crimes Squad, was scheduled for 28 September 1989, but was pulled that day a High Court judge granted the Police Federation an injunction preventing its screening for seven days. this squad had been involved with the case of the Birmingham Six. The injunction was based on the alleged risk of serious prejudice to forthcoming criminal proceedings. The BBC applied to the Court of Appeal, which on 30 September gave the go-ahead for the programme to be transmitted. It was shown on 26 October 1989.

October 1989 - BBC Northern Ireland
SPOTLIGHT
On 19 October 1989, *Spotlight* carried an interview with Tommy Little, a leader of the Ulster Defence Association. His voice was silenced and a reporter read an exact transcript of his words.

October 1989 - BBC
LATE SHOW
In a Late Show item on 9 October 1989 about the broadcasting ban, Sinn Fein councillor Mitchel McLaughlin was voiced over in sync by actor Harry Towb, who reproduced even the 'ums'. This had the strange effect of making McLaughlin, a Derry man in his early forties whose voice is familiar to listeners in the area, sound like a Belfast docker in his sixties.

October 1989 - Channel 4
MEDIA SHOW
In a *Media Show* programme on the broadcasting ban, shown on 15 October 1989, Derry Sinn Fein councillor Mitchel McLaughlin was silenced and subtitled.

19 October was the first anniversary of the introduction of the broadcasting ban.

October 1989 - Channel 4
HARD NEWS
In a *Hard News* item on media coverage of Ireland, shown on 19 October 1989, Danny Morrison, Sinn Fein's director of publicity, was silenced and subtitled.

October 1989 - BBC
QUESTION TIME
Jonathon Porritt and Paul Boateng MP recited the lyrics of the Pogues' song 'Birmingham Six' on *Question Time* on 19 October 1989. Unlike the IBA, the BBC had no ban on the song. Paul Boateng said, 'I felt it important to highlight the absurdity of the regulation,' and accused the IBA of 'cravenness' (*Sunday Correspondent*, 22 October 1989).

October 1989 - Channel 4
AFTER DARK
An *After Dark* programme on censorship, planned for 21 October 1989 and marking the first anniversary of the broadcasting ban, was scrapped with the IBA said it could not include members of organisations covered by the ban. The producers of the live late-night discussion programme had aimed to include Danny Morrison, publicity director of Sinn Fein, silencing his words and having a stand-in repeat them. An IBA spokesperson said, 'the voice-over method was thought unworkable in a live TV-interview situation. Technically, it might have been allowed, but in the context, it could have transgressed the guidelines' (*Sunday Correspondent*, 22 October 1989).

October 1989 - Channel 4
RIGHT TO REPLY
Two contributors to a *Right to Reply* programme on 28 october 1989 were voiced over. The first was Tony Doherty, a young man from Derry, who complained about the broadcasting ban in a 'videobox' item. Second to be voiced over was Mary Nelis, also from Derry, who participated in a studio

discussion in Belfast about the BBC's *Families at War* series. She was introduced with the words, 'Now, Mary, you're a member of Sinn Fein, so, we say again, people will not hear your voice.' She complained about the *Families at War* programme on ex-prisoner Shane Paul O'Doherty.

January 1990 - UTV
COUNTERPOINT
A *Counterpoint* programme on 18 January 1990 on the planned conference/concert hall for Belfast included an interview with Sinn Fein councillor Mairtin O Muilleoir, but without using his voice. O Muilleoir afterwards accused UTV of broadening the scope of the broadcasting ban. He said that a *Counterpoint* reporter had agreed his comments should be broadcast, but that his interview had subsequently been presented as one given by a representative of Sinn Fein rather than as by a councillor for Upper Falls. He pointed out that former Home Secretary Douglas Hurd had said Sinn Fein councillors could be interviewed if they were speaking as members of a council rather than as members of Sinn Fein (*Irish News*, 22 January 1990).

February 1990 - BBC
ON THE RECORD
Three Sinn Fein spokespersons were silenced and dubbed over by actors' voices in *On the Record* on 18 February 1990. The programme included an assessment of Northern Ireland Secretary Peter Brooke's current initiative. Those voiced over were Sinn Fein president Gerry Adams, Sinn Fein councillor Mairtin O Muilleoir, and party spokesperson Richard McAuley.

March 1990 - BBC Northern Ireland
MURDER OF SAMUEL MARSHALL
On 7 March 1990 Samuel Marshall was shot dead by loyalists as he walked away from a Lurgan police station where he reported as a condition of bail. Next day Sinn Fein held a press conference to be addressed by two witnesses to the killing, neither of whom were members of Sinn Fein. But while Ulster Television News carried comments by one of the men, the local BBC news did not broadcast either man's comments. Keith Baker, head of BBC news and current affairs for Northern Ireland, said: 'It was the BBC's view that the context of the news conference placed it within the terms of the restriction' (*Journalist*, May 1990).

April 1990 - UTV
THE STRUGGLE FOR DEMOCRACY
Ulster Television pulled this documentary made by Central Television from the schedule on 9 April 1990, when it was due to be shown, after four UDR

men were killed when a bomb blew up their landrover on the outskirts of Downpatrick. The programme included references to the Enniskillen Remembrance Day bombing and to Bloody Sunday in 1972. A UTV spokesman said that the film 'included some quite emotional passages and we felt it would have been insensitive to broadcast the programme in view of the tragic events of the day'. The programme was shown elsewhere on the ITV network on 9 April as scheduled.

April 1990 - Channel 4
DISPATCHES: 'Terms for Peace'
This *Dispatches* programme, by journalist Mary Holland, shown on 11 April 1990, included a 16-minute interview with Gerry Adams, MP for West Belfast and president of Sinn Fein. His voice was dubbed over in lip-sync by actor Stephen Rea. Leading republican Martin McGuinness was also dubbed in lip-sync. *Observer* TV reviewer John Naughton wrote that by this device, *Dispatches* 'drove a coach and horses through the Government's fatuous ban on Sinn Fein and other prohibited spokespersons' (*Observer*, 15 April 1990). *Guardian* reviewer Hugh Herbert wrote that it was 'the ultimate demonstration of the total stupidity of the ban' (*Guardian*, 12 April 1990).

June 1990 - UTV
SHOOT TO KILL
Ulster Television refused to screen *Shoot to Kill*, a four-hour documentary drama reconstructing the RUC killings of six unarmed men - five of them paramilitaries - in County Armagh in 1982. The programme, made by Yorkshire Television, was due to be screened throughout the ITV network on 3 and 4 June 1990. UTV claimed to be acting on legal advice, that to show the programme would be contempt of court. The Belfast *Irish News* suggested this might refer to a Court of Appeal hearing currently being brought by relatives of four of the dead, and commented that 'while the case is certainly "active", in view of the massive publicity which the 1982 shootings have generated over the years, during which there have been several related court cases, the UTV decision comes as something of a surprise' (*Irish News*, 1 June 1990).The Committee on the Administration of Justice, a Belfast-based pressure group, organised a screening of *Shoot to Kill* to an invited audience on 17 June at the Queen's Film Theatre.

July 1990
DEAR SARAH
Written by journalist Tom McGurk, *Dear Sarah* was a television drama based on the love story of Sarah Conlon and her husband Giuseppe Conlon, one of the 'Maguire Seven', arrested in 1974 and imprisoned for explosive offences.

Giuseppe Conlon had died of tuberculosis in 1980 in the hospital next to Wormwood Scrubs prison, still protesting his innocence, and was only vindicated in 1989 when the Guildford Four - one of whom was his son Gerry - were released.

McGurk originally wrote the script as a one-hour BBC drama in 1986, but the BBC rejected it. Then David Elstein at Thames TV recommissioned it as a 90-minute film, bringing in Frank Cvitanovich as director. The project then had a bumpy ride, first rejected by Thames TV's board - apparently unnerved by the *Death on the Rock* controversy in 1988 - then approved by them in the autumn of 1989, only to be vetoed again a month later. Thames had by now set up a co-production deal with RTE, the Irish broadcasting company. After Thames' withdrawal, RTE tried to interest Ulster Television and Channel 4, but without success. Finally RTE took over the entire production, financing it by pre-selling it to the ITV network. The finished film was shown on ITV on 2 July 1990.

'Time to Know' Campaign.
Blowing the Whistle outside MI5 HQ on the second anniversary of the ban.

July 1990 - Yorkshire
FIRST TUESDAY: Joyriders
In this programme on joyriders, shown on 3 July 1990, Alex Maskey of Sinn Fein was silenced and dubbed over by an actor's voice.

** July 1990 - Sky TV
NBC NIGHTLY NEWS: Interview with Richard McAuley
On 20 July 1990 the satellite channel Sky TV breached the broadcasting ban by transmitting an interview with Sinn Fein spokesperson Richard McAuley. He had been interviewed by the American *NBC Nightly News* programme, which Sky TV regularly transmits live at 11.30 pm. The director of programming of the Cable Authority, Tony Currie, said he would be raising the matter with Sky, and commented, 'This is an obvious breach of the authority's direction under the Cable and Broadcasting Act of 1984' (*Broadcast*, 27 July 1990).

On 7 September 1990, Mr Justice Carswell, a judge in the Northern Ireland High Court, refused an application by Sinn Fein councillor Mitchel McLaughlin for judicial review of the ban.

19 October was the second anniversary of the
introduction of the broadcasting ban

October 1990 - BBC and ITN
NEWS
On Sunday 30 September 1992, joyriders Martin Peake and Karen Reilly were shot dead by British soldiers in West Belfast. Next day, Gerry Adams, MP for the area, was interviewed by various TV and radio programmes, which varied in how they transmitted the interview. On BBC Radio 4's one o'clock news, Gerry Adams' words were spoken by a reporter, with the interviewer's questions inserted. But BBC television's six o'clock and nine o'clock news that evening carried Adams' own voice, saying, 'I will be asking how many shots were fired, why has no one seen the car, why don't the British Army put forward spokespersons, how many soldiers were involved?' (*Daily Mail*, 2 October 1992). By contrast ITN used a reporter to paraphrase Adams' words, stating, 'In comments which can't be broadcast under government restrictions, West Belfast MP Gerry Adams claimed the security forces knew the area was a race-track for joyriders'.

The BBC told the press it had taken legal advice before screening the interview, and that the broadcast did not contravene the guidelines because 'Mr Adams was speaking as MP for the constituency where one of the victims lived' (*Daily Mail*, 2 October 1990). Tory MP Ivor Stanbrook called the incident an 'outrageous breach' of the government's ban, and Democratic Unionist MP the Rev William McCrea also complained, but the Home Office said it would not investigate it (*Irish News*, 2 October 1990).

October 1990 - BBC
THE MARY WHITEHOUSE EXPERIENCE

According to the Sun, the BBC banned a comedy sketch of Terry Wogan 'dressed as an IRA terrorist' from the *Mary Whitehouse Experience* on the advice of its lawyers. The *Sun* wrote: 'The tasteless gag had a Wogan impressionist wearing a black balaclava, camouflage clothing and toting a machine gun' (*Sun*, 3 October 1990).

Second Anniversary of the Ban.
Liz Forgan of Channel 4 received an 'invoice' from Jake Ecclestone (NUJ) and Alan Sapper (ACTT) for legal costs incurred by the unions in their fight against the broadcasting ban.

October 1990 - BBC
STAR TREK

The *Daily Mail* speculated on 17 October 1990 that the BBC might censor a future series of *Star Trek*. The BBC bought a package of more than 80 episodes of *Star Trek* from its American makers. The *Mail* reported: 'In one episode, mention is made of British forces quitting Ulster in the 21st century after an IRA victory. "Characters refer to the Army pulling out because they couldn't win," a BBC insider revealed last night'. The episode was not due to be shown for the next couple of years'. Rumour has it that this episode was made in response to Irish American complaints about a previous edition featuring drunken, violent people with Irish accents! (Any information on this entry would be welcome! Please send it to the author, care of the publishers.)

October 1990 - Channel 4
TERROR: 'The Decay of Democracy'
The last episode of this three-part documentary series, transmitted on 29ᵗʰ October 1990, used an actor's voice to dub over Sinn Fein spokesperson Jim Gibney.

November 1990 - BBC
QUESTION TIME
The BBC pulled out of broadcasting *Question Time* from Belfast City Hall on 8 November 1990 because of the Unionist-dominated city council's policy not to allow British government ministers onto the premises - a protest against the Anglo-Irish Agreement of 1985. The programme was broadcast from Bradford instead.

November 1990 - BBC
INSIDE STORY: 'The Maze - Enemies Within'
The Maze - Enemies Within', transmitted on 20 November 1990, shoed the daily lives of republican and loyalist prisoners in the Maze prison, formerly Long Kesh. Where prisoners were speaking in a personal capacity, their own voices were heard, but where they were speaking as IRA representatives, their voices were dubbed by actors. One of those affected was the 'IRA spokesman on food': his words, spoken by an actor, were. 'Well, the thing about the sausage rolls ... they're getting smaller, in terms of size and all that there, y'know. The quality is still all right' (*Independent*, 21 November 1990).

February 1991 - BBC
CHILDREN OF THE NORTH
Children of the North, a four-part thriller set in the North of Ireland, was due to be shown in February 1991, but the BBC withdrew it because, in the words of the *Observer*, it decided 'it was inappropriate to air a programme whose theme was violence when British troops were fighting in the Gulf' (*Observer*, 27 October 1991). The series was finally shown in the autumn, starting on 30 October 1991.

** March 1991 - IBA
STREETS OF SORROW/BIRMINGHAM SIX'
The Belfast *Irish News* reported on 21 March 1991 that the IBA had lifted its ban on the Pogues' song 'Streets of Sorrow/Birmingham Six', which proclaimed the innocence of the Birmingham Six and Guildford Four. The IBA said, 'Now that the Birmingham Six are obviously not convicted terrorists, the record can be played again'.

April 1991 - Channel 4
'BANNED' SEASON
Channel Four ran a three-week season titled *Banned*, from 8 April 1991, featuring controversial television programmes. Several of these were on Ireland: *Mother Ireland, World in Action*'s 'The Propaganda War', *This Week*'s 'Death on the Rock', and *Dispatches*' interview with Gerry Adams. Ironically, every one of these was censored as a result of the broadcasting ban.

April 1991 - Channel 4
'BANNED' SEASON: Mother Ireland
This was the first screening for Derry Film & Video's *Mother Ireland*, which was the first television programme to be banned after the introduction of the broadcasting ban (see above, October/November 1988). *Mother Ireland* examines the relationship between women and Irish nationalism. Following the ban, it was shown at events and festivals in Britain and abroad, and on overseas television stations. It was widely acclaimed.

The version shown by Channel 4 in its *Banned* season, on 11 April 1991, was, however, itself censored. Some of the alterations were those demanded by Channel 4 before the introduction of the broadcasting ban. The programme-makers had to remove footage of Mrs Emma Groves filmed immediately after she had been shot in the face - and, as it turned out, blinded - by a rubber bullet in 1971: paradoxically this sequence had been shown by the BBC on 9 May 1989, in a short film for *Split Screen* by Ken Loach. They also had to remove Christy Moore's song *Unfinished Rewvolution*, and footage of a group of women in the IRA.

Additional changes were made because of the broadcasting ban. An interview with Mairead Farrell was dubbed over in lip-sync by an actress: Farrell was one of the three IRA members shot dead by the SAS in Gibraltar in 1988, and the interview had been filmed after her release from Armagh gaol. But an interview with Rita O'Hare, a leading Sinn Fein member in Dublin, was not voiced over: her affiliation was not mentioned, and she was simply captioned by her name.

April 1991 - Channel 4
RIGHT TO REPLY
Complaints about the censorship of *Mother Ireland* were voiced on *Right to Reply* on 13 April 1991. This programme repeated parts of the interview with Mairead Farrell dubbed over with an actress' voice. *Right to Reply* showed scenes from two sequences which had been cut from the programme: a group of women IRA members, and Mrs Emma Groves after she had been hit in the face by a rubber bullet.

April 1991 - Channel 4
'BANNED' SEASON: This Week: 'Death on the Rock'
Thames TV's 'Death on the Rock', which had provoked government fury by asking questions about the SAS killings of three IRA members in Gibraltar in March 1988, was shown for the second time on 18 April 1991, as part of Channel 4's *Banned* season.

But this screening, unlike the first one, was censored. Because of the broadcasting ban, Channel 4 replaced a sound recording of the voice of Mairead Farrell, one of the Gibraltar victims, with subtitles. Over a still photo of a house, the first caption read: 'It's all a political act even what happened in Enniskillen is a political act because it wouldn't have happened if Britain weren't in Ireland.' The second caption, referring to her arrest for a bombing offence in the 1970s, read: 'Nowadays they don't take prisoners. You know I was lucky, I was lucky.'

April 1991 - Channel 4
'BANNED' SEASON: World in Action: 'The Propaganda War'
This screening, on 23 April 1991, was the first for Granada's 'The Propaganda War', made during the 1981 hunger strikes. Granada withdrew the film in June 1981 rather than comply with the IBA's command to excise a 27-second sequence showing hunger striker Patsy O'Hara in his coffin. (See chronology in *Ireland: The Propaganda War*, p.289.)

For this screening, the disputed sequence was reinstated, but, because of the broadcasting ban, Sinn Fein spokesman Joe Austin was dubbed over by an actor in lip-sync, as was an H Block blanket protester, who shouted, 'We're political prisoners. We want political status'. The H Block sequence had been shown intact on television in 1981.

April 1991 - Channel 4
'BANNED' SEASON: Dispatches: 'Terms for Peace'
This showing, on 22 April 1991, was a repeat of the *Dispatches* programme which included a long interview with Gerry Adams MP, meticulously dubbed over in lip-sync by actor Stephen Rea. The programme was previously shown on 11 April 1990 (see above).

June 1991 - BBC Northern Ireland
SPOTLIGHT: The Official IRA
The Irish Republican Socialist Party claimed that BBC governors in Britain had pressurised the *Spotlight* team to drop this programme, which featured claims that the Official IRA (in theory disbanded) had carried out racketeering, fraud and armed robberies, and that some of those convicted of such crimes

were members of the Workers Party (formerly Official Sinn Fein).

Kevin McQuillan, a spokesperson for the IRSP, which split from the Officials, claimed that the programme had been scheduled for May 1991, then rescheduled for 13 June, then stopped again. The BBC rejected allegations of pressure either from the BBC or from the Northern Ireland Office to stop the programme. It was finally shown on 27 June 1991 (*Irish News*, 14 June, 28 June 1991).

19 October was the third anniversary of the
introduction of the broadcasting ban

** In October 1991 the Independent Television Commission (replacement of the IBA) refused to renew the franchise of Thames Television. This was widely seen as a punishment for Thames for showing 'Death on the Rock', about the SAS killings in Gibraltar, in 1988.

A Channel 4 *Dispatches* programme, alleging high-level RUC involvement in a loyalist committee which planned the murder of Catholics, led to a long-running battle between the RUC and Channel 4. Made by Box Productions, the programme was transmitted on 2 October 1991. The RUC investigated, and the Metropolitan Police Special Branch obtained orders under the Prevention of Terrorism Act requiring Channel 4 and Box Productions to hand over files and other materials relating to the programme. Both companies refused to comply with the orders, because they had promised a source - known as 'Source A' - that they would protect his identity. Instead, they destroyed or sent abroad material that could have compromised him. Channel 4 and Box Productions were then charged with contempt of court, and on 31 July 1992 were fined £75,000. There was relief that the fine was relatively low, but concern that the judgement denied programme-makers the right to give an unqualified undertaking to a source to protect their anonymity.

Two months later, on 29 September 1992, the researcher for the programme, Ben Hamilton, was arrested at his home in London. He was held for questioning, then charged with perjury. The charges were dropped two months later.

November 1991 - BBC
OMNIBUS: 'Ulster Says Ho Ho Ho'
Ninety seconds of a comedian's Ian Paisley routine were cut from this programme on humour in the North of Ireland, and the majority of his expletives were bleeped. The *Independent* reported: 'The BBC claims legal

reasons for the changes ... while other sources hold BBC Northern Ireland responsible' (*Independent*, 19 November 1991).

January 1992 - Channel 4

FREE FOR ALL: '20 Years After Bloody Sunday'

This programme included an interview with Raymond McCartney, captioned 'Officer Commanding Republican Prisoners, Maze Prison', who was, as the second caption put it, 'Re-voiced due to government broadcasting restrictions'.

** During the spring 1992 general election campaign, Unionist politicians in the North of Ireland adopted a ploy to deny Sinn Fein air time. Under the terms of the Representation of the People Act, the broadcasting ban cannot be applied during elections. But Unionists found they were able to silence Sinn Fein by themselves refusing to appear, because under electoral law all candidates or none have to be interviewed (*Independent*, 21 March 1992; *Irish News*, 27 March 1992).

March 1992 - BBC Radio 4

AFTERNOON STORY: 'We've Got Tonite' by Danny Morrison

The BBC banned a short story by former Sinn Fein publicity director Danny Morrison, currently imprisoned in Long Kesh, from being read on Radio 4's *Afternoon Story* slot. Titled 'We've Got Tonite', the story was an innocuous tale of suburban love and adultery, with no mention of Ireland, and with no political content. The story was recorded in February 1992, and was due for transmission on 12 March. Danny Morrison then received a letter saying it had been postponed. Further enquiries produced a letter from BBC Belfast stating that the broadcasting of the story would be 'inappropriate' and that there would be no payment. Morrison wrote again asking for explanation and guidance, because the previous year, in reply to an enquiry from him, Radio 5 had encouraged him to write a play. He received a letter, dated 22 September 1992, from John Wilson, the BBC's Controller of Editorial Policy. Wilson wrote: 'The problem is your close connection with terrorism, not criminal conviction as a generality. It would be inappropriate to have a broadcast for entertainment purposes based on your work when so many people are victims of terrorism and so many more detest and fear it. Many people would be deeply offended.

In view of that your short story should never have been accepted and in the existing circumstances you should forget any encouragement from anywhere in the BBC to write a play or other creative work for entertainment purposes' (see also the *Guardian*, 14 October 1992).

** June 1992 - Sky TV
HIDDEN AGENDA

On 29 June 1992, Sky TV, the satellite company owned by Rupert Murdoch, screened Ken Loach's *Hidden Agenda* uncut to European viewers. The film, loosely based on the Stalker shoot-to-kill enquiry and the Colin Wallace affair, includes a scene where a real life Sinn Fein Councillor, Jim McAllister, plays a fictitious Sinn Fein member. Ken Loach had said the previous year: 'Here you have a Sinn Fein councillor playing a Sinn Fein member espousing Sinn Fein policy. It'll be interesting to see how broadcasters in Britain and Ireland cope with it' (*Irish News*, 1 July 1992).

September 1992 - BBC
NATION: 'Killing for a Cause'

The BBC provoked widespread protests when it extensively subtitled the contribution of former MP Bernadette Devlin McAliskey to a pre-recorded discussion in the *Nation* series, transmitted on 1 September 1992. Other participants were also subtitled, including 77-year-old Brent trade unionist Tom Durkin. None of those subtitled was a member or representative of organisations covered by the broadcasting ban.

The gist of Bernadette McAliskey's contribution was that while she did not support violence, she understood the reasons for it. She said, for example: 'No sane human being supports violence. We are often inevitably cornered into it by powerlessness, by lack of democracy, by lack of willingness of people to listen to our problems. We don't choose political violence, the powerful force it on us".

The programme was made by Juniper Productions for the BBC's multicultural unit, based in Birmingham. The executive producer was David Cox, who in 1990 had produced *Dispatches'* 'Terms for Peace', which had achieved some notoriety by featuring a long interview with Gerry Adams dubbed in lip-sync by actor Stephen Rea (see above, April 1990).

Exactly how and why the *Nation* programme was subtitled remains a matter of dispute and speculation. The programme-makers had originally considered a number of other interviewees, including Gerry Adams and Martin McGuinness, both of whom would have had to be subtitled or re-voiced under the terms of the broadcasting ban.

There are suspicions that the programme-makers 'set Bernadette up', planning in advance to subtitle her, but they deny this. Inexperience in relations to Ireland on the part of the BBC's multicultural unit and the BBC's duty lawyers may have played a part.

Before recording started, the participants were reassured that subtitling was unlikely. But when recording began, Trevor Phillips' introduction included this warning: 'A government order made in 1988 requires broadcasters to remove the sound when something is said which could be taken as supporting certain organisations involved in the Northern conflict, such as the Provisional IRA and the Ulster Defence Association. To comply with this order, we'll use subtitles when necessary'. Juniper Productions then edited the programme down from about 90 minutes to just under 40. They did not include Trevor Phillips' warning in the first version because they did not think it would be necessary.

The programme was recorded on 23 August and transmitted nine days later, on 1 September. Bernadette McAliskey only learned about the subtitling by an indirect route on the evening of 31 August. Next day, through solicitor Gareth Peirce, Bernadette made strenuous efforts to get the BBC to withdraw the programme or, failing that, to remove the subtitles or to remove her contribution, but to no avail. Gareth Peirce wrote to the BBC that the subtitling was defamatory, and that 'the clearest possible implication' of the subtitles 'as is spelled out by the presenter Trevor Phillips in the introduction … is that either she or the words spoken by her lend support to the views and actions of proscribed organisations. This is most clearly not the position of Ms McAliskey and was not the view that she put forward on the programme'.

Trade unionist Tom Durkin also tried to get his contribution deleted, but was repeatedly fobbed off by BBC information officers. Various civil liberties organisations made protests about the extension of the ban. Following transmission, the BBC was inundated with telephone calls of protest.

On 3 September Conservative MP Peter Bottomley, who had appeared on the programme alongside Bernadette, wrote to Sir Michael Checkland, Director-General of the BBC, describing the BBC's action as 'defamatory and dangerous for Bernadette'.

On 7 September the BBC's then Controller of Editorial Policy, John Wilson, returned from holiday and was very annoyed to discover what had happened. His view apparently was that the BBC should apologise to Bernadette and retransmit the programme without subtitles. This, however, annoyed the BBC's lawyers, who were upset at the criticism of their line. The apparently got together to protest. Faced with conflicting pressures, Director-General Sir Michael Checkland brought in an outside lawyer, David Pannick, to adjudicate. Pannick concluded, in the words of a BBC statement, 'that it was right to subtitle all of Ms McAliskey's main remarks at the beginning of the programme but that it need not have subtitled her much shorter closing remarks' (BBC statement, 14 September 1992). Pannick's conclusions suggest that he thought the context into which the programme had put Bernadette was a key element in justifying the subtitling. He felt the broadcasting ban applied to her because, firstly, she was 'introduced as a past supporter of Irish republicanism and violence', and, secondly, she had said she could understand and explain the violence 'in the context of three specific bomb outrages involving the Provisional IRA'. In fact, each of these bomb outrages had been mentioned to her by the presenter, Trevor Phillips.

Subsequently Bernadette McAliskey - with solicitor Gareth Peirce acting on her behalf - applied for a judicial review of the BBC's action. This was refused by Mr Justice MacPherson, who ruled that a judicial review was not a correct remedy and that she should take an action for defamation. Bernadette then applied to the court of appeal, which in July 1993 overturned MacPherson's decision and gave her leave to obtain the review. The three appeal court judges - Master of the Rolls Sir Thomas Bingham, and Lord Justices Steyn and Waite - said it was at least arguable that the BBC's interpretation of the 1988 directive raised a 'serious and substantial' question of law. For its part, the BBC stated, 'The restrictions are an improper interference with freedom of speech. The BBC has opposed them from the very start and we continue to do so' (*Irish News*, 22 July 1993).

September 1992 - BBC
BITEBACK: Bernadette Ban
On 17 September 1992 *Biteback*, which airs criticisms of BBC programmes, included a report on the 'Bernadette ban' affair. It featured interviews with John Wilson, Tom Durkin, David Cox, journalist Peter Taylor and David Miller of the Glasgow University Media Group. Bernadette McAliskey declined to be interviewed because she feared she might be subtitled again.

Biteback used extracts from the offending interview with Bernadette, with subtitles and missing voice, and also similarly dubbed footage of Tom Durkin and another member of the audience. The programme contrasted the subtitling episode with footage of Bernadette participating in an *Open to Question* discussion on 3 February 1992, saying something very similar but without interference with her voice.

Biteback also repeated a section of *Inside Story: Enemies Within*, about Long Kesh prison (aka The Maze), in which the IRA spokesperson on food was both subtitled and re-voiced by an actor as he discussed the quality of the sausage rolls.

88

October 1992 - BBC
EASTENDERS
Scriptwriter David Yallop lost his job on the television series *Eastenders* in November 1989 after he proposed killing off several members of the cast in an IRA bombing. He sued the BBC for breach of contract, and on 17 October 1992 won £68,195 High Court damages plus interest. The award represented money owed to him. The BBC faced a legal bill unofficially estimated at £250,000. Yallop accused the BBC of 'a total lack of balls'. He told the press: 'We live in incredible times, thousands of workers losing their jobs each week, homeless people on the streets, eight bombs in eight days. Where is that reflected in BBC drama?' (*Independent*, 17 October 1992).

19 October was the fourth anniversary of the
introduction of the broadcasting ban

** To mark the fourth anniversary of the broadcasting ban, Sinn Fein defiantly breached the ban by openly running a pirate radio station in West Belfast on Saturday 17 October 1992. The *Irish News* reported:

'Radio Free Sinn Fein, which could be picked up in most parts of Belfast on 106FM from 11 am to 4 pm, was broadcast from a purpose-built stage in Andersonstown. Sinn Fein members acted as DJs, reading out requests and playing music. Interviews were carried out with various party officials, including president Gerry Adams.

'A "Sinn Fein Radio Roadshow" was set up in conjunction with the broadcast. Children played on a bouncy castle in Avoca Park and took part in radio competitions' (*Irish News*, 19 October 1992).

October 1992 - BBC Northern Ireland and UTV
SINN FEIN STATEMENT
Writing in the *Irish News*, Sinn Fein president Gerry Adams complained that: 'On Tuesday, October 20, the Church of Ireland Primate, Dr Eames, in a speech to his Synod, strongly criticised myself as Sinn Fein president.

News management of Sinn Fein material ensured that neither BBC nor UTV carried any response from Sinn Fein on their evening news reports.

When contacted, the BBC reported that the statement had been "lost".

'If Dr Eames had made a similar outspoken criticism of the SDLP or Unionists, it would be unthinkable that they would not have been given an opportunity to respond - in fact the BBC would have gone looking for a response!' (*Irish News*, 10 November 1992)

October 1992 - BBC West
HERE ACROSS THE WATER
'Here Across the Water' was a documentary which traced the links between Ireland and Bristol by looking at the lives of four Irishwomen living in Bristol, of different ages and interests. The film was originally scheduled to go out in October 1992 during the Bristol Irish Festival, but was then postponed to 18 March 1993, the day after St Patrick's Day - not a move that the programme-makers approved of, because they felt that Irish material should not be ghettoised. The BBC publicised the date, as did the Bristol Irish Society - but the programme was pulled again, as the last minute, to make way for a story on local job losses at Rolls Royce.

After pressure from the local Irish community, the programme was finally shown on 29 April 1993, but the Bristol Irish Society found it difficult to publicise it effectively because this was the third time the programme had been promised. As a result, the follow-up phone-in on radio was something of a damp squib.

January 1993 - BBC
TIMEWATCH: 'The sparks that lit the bonfire'
This programme, shown on 23 January 1993, looked at the early days of the 'troubles' and the possible role of the Irish government in the formation of the Provisional IRA. It revealed a rather curious voiceover policy - two people each ended up speaking with two voices, one their own and the other an actor's. An early sound recording of IRA leader Sean MacStiofain saying 'concessions be damned - we want freedom' was voiced over by an actor, but in an interview done for the programme, MacStiofain's own voice was used. Part of an interview done for the programme with Joe Cahill, former Belfast commander of the IRA, was used without interfering with his voice - when he was talking about the split between the Official and Provisional IRA; but part was voiced over - when he was talking about the Provisionals' military campaign. A short clip of Gerry Adams giving a speech was also voiced over.

** On 3 March 1993, BBC Wales gave the first British television screening to *Hang Up Your Brightest Colours*, Kenneth Griffith's long-banned documentary on the life and death of Michael Collins, a hero of the Irish war of independence of 1919-21. The film was banned in 1973 by ATV.

March 1993 - Channel 4
HIDDEN AGENDA
Ken Loach's award-winning feature film *Hidden Agenda*, about sinister undercover operations by the British state in the North of Ireland, was scheduled to have its first mainstream British television screening on 21 March

1993. (It had previously been shown on Sky TV on 29 June 1992 - see above.) But after the IRA's bombing in Warrington the day before, when a child was killed, Channel 4 decided to pull the programme, and was inundated with protesting telephone calls. Ken Loach told the press: 'Provided it didn't offend people's grief there's no reason to ban it. We have got to discuss the issues openly. The horrific events in Warrington were awful beyond words but people talk about it as though it bears no relation to British practices in Northern Ireland. Foremost among the men of violence are the British' (*Guardian*, 23 March 1993).

Hidden Agenda was eventually shown on 16 April 1993.

March 1993 - Channel 4
ANGEL
Angel, a non-realistic thriller set in the North of Ireland directed by Neil Jordan and starring Stephen Rea, was first shown on Channel 4 on 15 November 1984. It was scheduled to be repeated on 23 March 1993 but was pulled by Channel 4 in the wake of Warrington. Sources at Channel 4 said that the only reason it was pulled was that *Hidden Agenda* was being pulled, and to allow *Angel* to go ahead might have provoked allegations of double standards. It was finally shown on 8 June 1993.

** During the May 1993 local election campaign, Sinn Fein in Belfast broadcast pirate radio programmes on 'SFFM'. Technically this was not a breach of the broadcasting ban, which does not apply during election periods because it would contravene the Representation of the People Act.

June 1993 - BBC Scotland
AXIOM
Sinn Fein councillor Mairtin O Muilleoir was among the panellists on the BBC Scotland discussion programme, *Axiom*, about the North of Ireland and its significance for Scotland. The programme was recorded on 3 June and shown the following day, with O Muilleoir's voice dubbed over by an actor's. Mairtin O Muilleoir subsequently received a substantial sum in an out of court settlement from the *Sunday Express*, which had published an article complaining about an 'IRA councillor' being brought to Scotland at the expense of the BBC (*Irish News*, 29 July 1993).

July 1993 - Channel 4
FRONTLINE
On 3 July 1993 *Frontline* featured a film by Belfast journalist Malachi O'Doherty about how the inquest system fails people whose relatives have been killed by the British army or Royal Ulster Constabulary. The voice of Sinn Fein spokesperson Richard McAuley was dubbed over by an actor's.

ACKNOWLEDGEMENTS

Thanks to Helen Dady, David Miller and many more who have given information over the years.

Liz Curtis, October 1993

8 Cynthia Stree, London, N1 9JF. Tel: 071 278 4430. Fax: 071 837 8868

CAMPAIGN OBJECTS

The Campaign for Press and Broadcasting Freedom was launched in 1979 to campaign for diverse, democratic and representative media. It has the support of 27 national trade unions and numerous branches, Constituency Labour Parties and individual members. The Campaign's objects are:

To challenge the myths of 'impartiality' and 'balance' in broadcasting and 'objectivity' in newspapers by campaigning for the genuine presentation of the diversity and plurality of society.

To challenge the myth that only private ownership of the newspaper industry provides genuine freedom, diversity or access.

To challenge the myth that the present forms of ownership and regulation of broadcasting guarantee editorial independence, democratic accountability or high programme standards.

To carry out research and generate debate on alternative forms of ownership and control of newspapers and broadcasting in order to guarantee freedom from either state control or domination by business conglomerates, and encourage the creation of alternative media including those sympathetic to the labour movement.

To work for press and broadcasting that are free of materials detrimental to any individual or group on the grounds of gender, race, class, religion, sexual preference, age or physical or mental ability; and to seek equality of opportunity and achievement in the media for disadvantaged groups.

To encourage debate on the implications of technology advances in the media, to ensure that the public interest is safeguarded and that commercial interests do not override public accountability.

To campaign on the general principles in the Minority Report of the 1977 Royal Commission on the Press, including proposals for a National Printing Corporation to provide a competitive public sector in the industry and a launch fund to assist new publications.

To campaign for the replacement of the Press Complaints Commission and the Broadcasting Complaints Commission with a statutory based Media Commission with power to receive complaints and enforce the right of reply, and promote basic standards of fairness and access to the media on behalf of the public. The Right of Reply is fundamental to redressing inaccuracies and bias.

To campaign for a reduction in the legal restrictions on freedom of publication and increased access to information through a Freedom of Information Bill and reform of the Official Secrets Act and similar restrictive legislation.

To campaign for the legal right of access for publications to the distribution system, and a guaranteed right of display.